MEL BAY'S COMPLETE JAZZ BASS BOOK

By Earl Gately

1 2 3 4 5 6 7 8 9 0

Visit us on the Web at http://www.melbay.com — E-mail us at email@melbay.com

Preface

Please read thoroughly the "Table of Contents" as they explain fully the philosophy and content of this method.

Recommended approach: Begin immediately studying the "Theory for the Bassist" (Part IV) as it contains all of the musical nomenclature so necessary for reading and interpreting chord symbols for jazz or any other type of music. Also, begin doing the ear development studies (intervals) (Part IV). These theory studies will relate to the scale and arpeggio (chords) studies in Part II, fifteen of the most essential and commonly used scales and the chords they generate. (Scale degrees and fingerings are given for each).

The above theory and scale studies are most important, as Part V, chord progressions show how to create bass lines by having a thorough knowledge of scale degrees.

Scale degrees are heavily emphasized in the Part V chord progressions, thus giving you, the bassist, the necessary tools to bring into being your own creative self whether it be rhythm section or soloing.

For the bassist who is a beginner or the bassist with minimal reading skills and just a vague knowledge of all the note locations on the bass, a very concentrated study of the first position is strongly recommended as this will methodically and thoroughly prepare the player to approach the following studies. Please read "Table of Contents" Part I.

Chord symbols are given over all of the very diverse bass lines, syncopated patterns, scales and arpeggios, etc. from the first chart excerpt in 1st position to the completion of the method.

Therefore, all the musical content contained herein is applicable to virtually any type of performing situation. The wider your range, the better musician you are, jazz or otherwise.

Thank you, and God bless,
Earl Gately

Earl Gately has had extensive performing experience in such diversified areas as jazz festivals, featuring such artists as Dennis Diblasio, Anthony Garcia, John Fedchock, etc., to Opryland in Nashville, two full-time symphony orchestras, many combos, and big bands. Currently, he teaches both Electric and String Bass (jazz and classical) at Bradley University and Knox College and formerly at Western Illinois University. Briefly summed up, Earl has a complete range of musical experience and continues actively as a performer.

Contents

Progressions I IV V

Part VI

Hand Positions
Proper Hand Position Is Essential For Good Technique

LEFT HAND POSITION*
This method uses the 1-2-3-4 fingering. Notice the placement of the fingers directly behind frets.

RIGHT HAND POSITION
Always alternate fingers 1 and 2 pulling straight across the string. Finger techniques are: using tip of finger pad, using the fingernail, and using the pad and fingernail together.

BACK VIEW OF HAND POSITION
Note position of thumb on the neck and its placement in relation to the fingers.

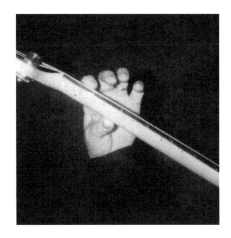

THE THUMB PIVOT, LOWER POSITION
This eliminates unnecessary shifts. This is done by rolling on the thumb and using the first or fourth finger to play a note in a lower or higher position without changing position and then rolling back on thumb to continue playing position.

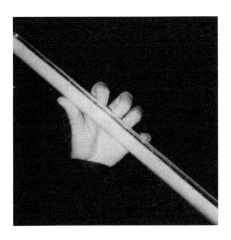

THE THUMB PIVOT, HIGHER POSITION
*A note on the left hand fingering. When depressing a note with the 2nd finger, also hold the 1st finger down. When depressing a note with the 3rd finger, hold the 1st and 2nd fingers down. When depressing a note with the 4th finger, hold the 1st, 2nd and 3rd fingers down.

Basic Theory

Types of Notes

| Whole Note | Half Notes | Quarter Notes | Eight Notes | Sixteenths Notes |
| 4 beats | 2 beats | 1 beat | 1/2 beat | 1/4 beat |

Types of Rests

| Whole Rest | Half Rest | Quarter Rest | Eight Rest | Sixteenths Rest |
| 4 beats | 2 beats | 1 beat | 1/2 beat | 1/4 beat |

Time Signatures: Consist of Upper Numbers (indicate number of beats per measure) and Lower Numbers (type of note that receives one beat or count

Measure   Bar Lines

Referred to as four four time. There are 4 quarter notes per measure.

Means *common* time. It is the same as 4/4 time.

Referred to as three four time. There are three quarter notes per measure.

Referred to as two four time. There are two quarter notes per measure.

Means *cut* time, called **alla breve**. There are two half notes per measure.

Basic Theory

The Dot: Placed after a note increases its value by one half.

             A half note gets 2 beats   A dotted half note gets 3 beats

The Tie: Ties on note of the same pitch into another. The first note is played and held down for the duration of the second note.

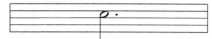

           count: 1   2   3   1   2   3

Sharps and Flats: Placed before note to raise or lower their pitch.

      Raises the note   Lowers the note   Raises the note   Lowers the note
      one half step   one half step   two half steps   two half steps

Accidental: Is a natural, sharp or flat which is foreign to the key, and lasts only for the measure in which it appears.

Natural: Cancels the sharp or flat; restores note to original pitch.

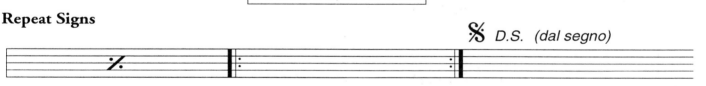

Repeat Signs

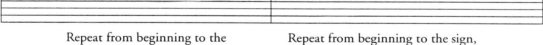

      Repeat previous   Repeat music between   Repeat to the sign and end
         measure   these two signs   at the word *Fine*

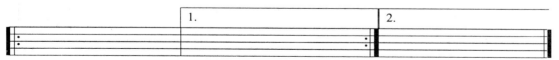

      Repeat from beginning to the   Repeat from beginning to the sign,
            word *Fine*   then go to *Coda*

                           Play through first ending, repeat passage,
                        skip first ending and play second ending.

First Position
How to Learn Notes and Fingering
This Procedure Can Be Applied For All Positions

First, look at the diagram, starting on the G string, SAY, PLAY, and LISTEN to the notes. After you know the notes and fingerings, look at the written notes in the box. Learn the location on the musical staff, and proceed to "playing on the G string". This is the test: whether or not you know the notes. If you cannot play the notes, study the diagram and box notes again. Follow this same procedure on all four strings. After studying "Notes on the string", set the Metronome at 60 (♩ = 60). This tempo will be your "GOAL" for the "Playing on the string" studies. When this GOAL is accomplished, move on to the next string.

8

Chord Symbol Notation, Type and Scale Degrees

Chord Type	Scale Degrees Used	Symbols
Major	Root, 3rd, 5th	Maj
Minor	Root, b3rd, 5th	mi,−,m
Diminished	Root, b3rd, b5th, bb7th (6)	dim,°
Augmented	Root, 3rd, #5th	+, aug.
Dominant Seventh	Root, 3rd, 5th, b7th	dom. 7, 7
Minor Seventh	Root, b3rd, 5th, b7th	−7, min 7
Major Seventh	Root, 3rd, 5th, maj. 7th	M7, ma 7, Δ7
Major Sixth	Root, 3rd, 5th, 6th	M6, M6, 6
Minor Sixth	Root, b3rd, 5th, 6th	mi 6,−6
Seventh #5th	Root, 3rd, #5th, b7th	7+5, 7#5
Seventh b5th	Root, 3rd, b5th, b7th	7-5, 7b5
Minor Major 7th	Root, b3rd, 5th, maj. 7th	m Δ7, −Δ7
Minor 7th b5th, Half Diminished	Root, b3rd, b5th, b7th	mi 7-5, −7b5, ø
Seventh Suspended 4th	Root, 4th, 5th, b7th	7 sus 4
Ninth	Root, 3rd, 5th, b7th, 9th	9
Minor Ninth	Root, b3rd, 5th, b7th, 9th	mi 9, −9
Major Ninth	Root, 3rd, 5th, maj. 7th, 9th	Ma 9
Ninth Augmented 5th	Root, 3rd, #5th, b7th, 9th	9+5, 9#5
Ninth Flatted 5th	Root, 3rd, b5th, b7th, 9th	9-5, 9b5
Seventh b9	Root, 3rd, 5th, b7th, b9th	7-9, 7, b9
Augmented Ninth (raised nine)	Root, 3rd, 5th, b7th, #9th	9+, 7#9
9/6	Root, 3rd, 5th, 6th, 9th	$\frac{9}{6}$, 6 add 9
Eleventh	Root, 3rd, 5th, b7th, 9th, 11th	11
Augmented Eleventh	Root, 3rd, 5th, b7th, 9th, #11th	11+, 7 aug 11
Thirteenth	Root, 3rd, 5th, b7th, 9th, 11th, 13th	13
Thirteenth b9	Root, 3rd, 5th, b7th, b9th, 11th, 13th	13b9
Thirteenth b9b5	Root, 3rd, b5th, b7th, b9th, 11th, 13th	13b9b5
Half Diminished	Root, b3rd, b5th, b7th	ø

Note—To arrive at scale degrees above 1 octave (i.e. 9th, 11th. 13th) continue your scale up 2 octaves and keep numbering. The 2nd scale degree will be the 9th tone as you begin your second octave, the 4th the 11th, and the 6th the 13th

First Position

Note Review: The chromatic scale in first position (sharps ascending, flats descending)

Look to Note Review: If experiencing any difficulty in remembering note names, fret location and fingerings while studying these,

CHART EXCERPTS

First Position
Scales in First Position

E Major Scales

E Blues Scales

A Major Scales

A Blues Scales

CHART EXCERPTS

1

2 Play with "2 Feel"

3 ♪♪ = to be played ♪³♪

11

Fingerboard Positions and Note Location Chart to the 12th Fret

This Unique Fingerboard Chart shows, in one glance, musical notation and what fret the note is located on. The Positions are numbered according to what fret the 1st finger is placed on. Example: When the 1st finger is placed on the 1st fret, you are in 1st position. When the 1st finger is placed on the 2nd fret, you are in 2nd position.

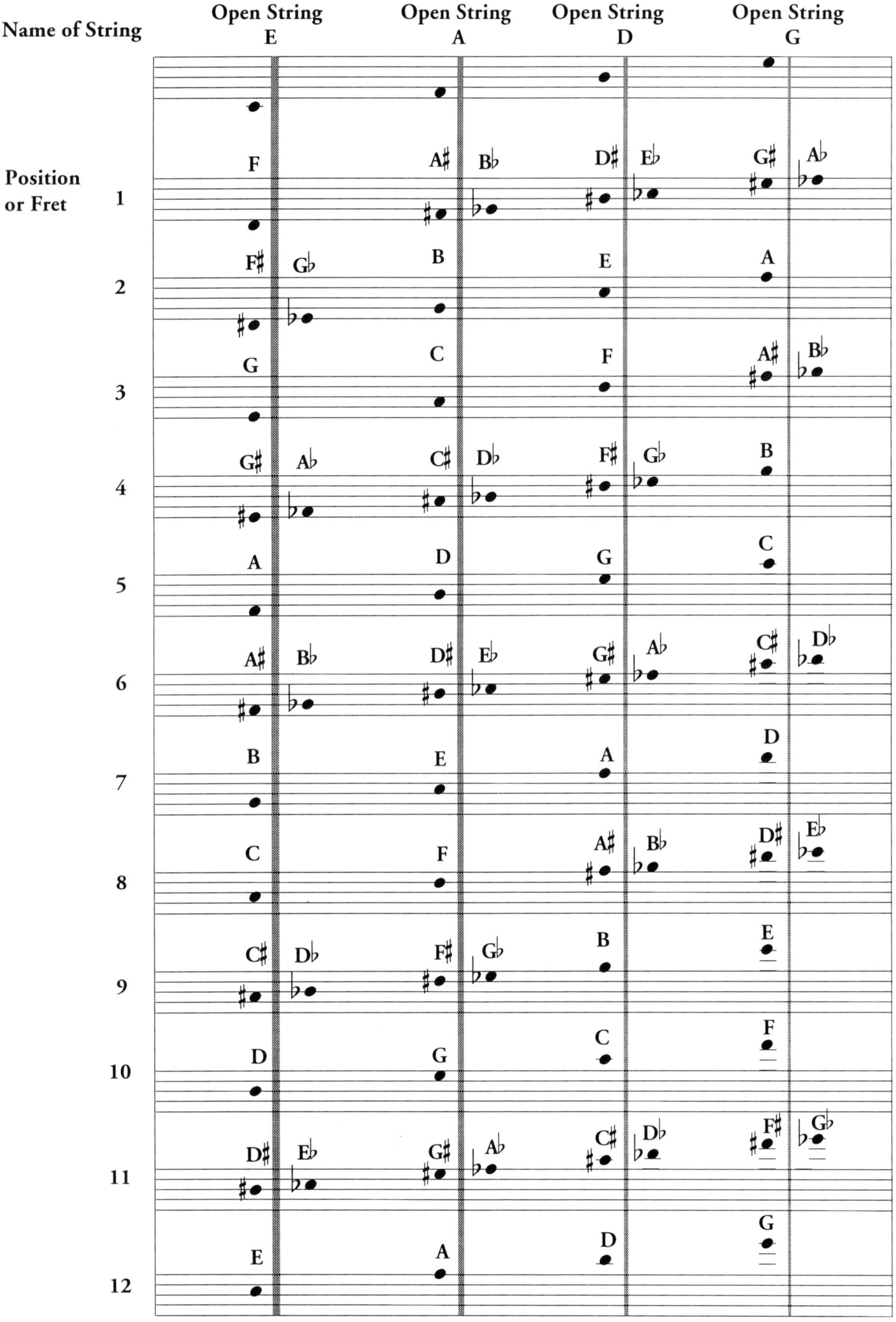

Position or Fret	Open String E	Open String A	Open String D	Open String G
Open	E	A	D	G
1	F	A♯ / B♭	D♯ / E♭	G♯ / A♭
2	F♯ / G♭	B	E	A
3	G	C	F	A♯ / B♭
4	G♯ / A♭	C♯ / D♭	F♯ / G♭	B
5	A	D	G	C
6	A♯ / B♭	D♯ / E♭	G♯ / A♭	C♯ / D♭
7	B	E	A	D
8	C	F	A♯ / B♭	D♯ / E♭
9	C♯ / D♭	F♯ / G♭	B	E
10	D	G	C	F
11	D♯ / E♭	G♯ / A♭	C♯ / D♭	F♯ / G♭
12	E	A	D	G

Name of String

Accelerated Fingerboard Study
First to Ninth Position

Playing and **Learning** the notes on each string up to the 12th fret. **Saying** and **Playing** is a great aid in remembering.
Shift hand on circle notes ① Left Hand Finger, ⑤ Position.

Accelerated Individual String Studies
First to Ninth Position

Each string has a different type minor scale, followed by a study using only the notes in the scale above it. Start right now hearing the subtle differences each of the scales produce, as they are used for rhythm section and solo playing.

You are learning your fingerboard, SAY, PLAY and LISTEN.

STUDY: FINGERBOARD AND NOTE LOCATION CHART TO THE 12TH FRET

14

Eighth Note Rhythm Studies

EIGHT REST

15

Triplet Rhythm Studies

A **Triplet** ia a group of three notes having the same time value as one quarter note or two eighth notes.

Say &
Play   tri - po - let   2 - po - let   3 - po - let   4 - po - let

Say &
Play   1   2   3- po- let 4   1   2   3- po- let 4   1   2- po- let 3   4

Say   1   2-po-let   3   4-po-let   1   2-po-let   3-po-let   4   1-po-let   2   3   4
Play 1   2 - let   3   4 - let   1   2 - let   3 - let   4   1 - let   2   3   4

TRIPLET STUDY

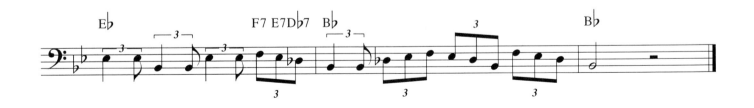

16

Sixteenth Note Rhythm Studies

How to figure out syncopated rhythm patterns: Think in 16th notes throughout the pattern. Use alternating fingering for right hand. These studies are a MUST in order to read modern bass charts.

Dotted Eighth and Sixteenth Notes

Say	1 A an A 2 A an A 3 A an A 4 A an A	1 A an A 2 A an A 3 A an A 4 A an A
Play	1 A an A 2 A an A 3 A an A 4 A an A	1 —— A 2 —— A 3 —— A 4 —— A

PLAY ALL THESE STUDIES - STRING A, FRET 5

Combining Eighth and Sixteenth Notes

Say	1 A an A 2 A an A 3 A an A 4 A an A	1 A an A 2 A an A 3 A an A 4 A an A
Play	1 — an A 2 — an A 3 — an A 4 — an A	1 A an — 2 A an — 3 A an — 4 A an —

Rhythm Patterns
Using sixteenth notes. eighth notes, dotted eighth and sixteenth note rests

1

Say	1 A an A 2 A an A 3 A an A 4 A an A	1 A an A 2 A an A 3 A an A 4 A an A
Play	1 —————— —— A 3 A —— — A an A	1 —————— — A 3 A an — — A an —

2

Say	1 A an A 2 A an A 3 A an A 4 A an A	1 A an A 2 A an A 3 A an A 4 A an A
Play	1 A an — 2 — A 3 —— A 4 A an —	1 —— A 2 A — A 3 A an — 4 A ——

3

4

Say	1 A an A 2 A an A 3 A an A 4 A an A
Play	1 A — A 2 A — A 3 A — A 4 A — A

5

Tie and Rhythm Studies

These studies are a MUST in order to read modern bass charts.

PLAY ALL THESE STUDIES - STRING A, FRET 5

Always use Alternating Fingering

Rhythm Patterns

Using ties

Second Position

Notes, frets, and fingerings for second position on all four strings

On the "G" string

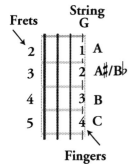

Note:	A	A♯	B♭	B	C
Finger:	1	2		3	4

| Fret: | 2 | 3 | 4 | 5 |

On the "D" string

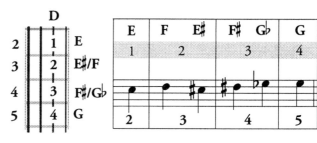

	E	F	E♯	F♯	G♭	G
	1	2		3		4

| | 2 | 3 | 4 | 5 |

On the "A" string

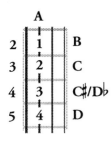

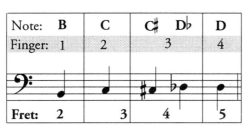

Note:	B	C	C♯	D♭	D
Finger:	1	2	3		4

| Fret: | 2 | 3 | 4 | 5 |

On the "E" string

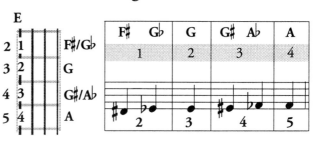

	F♯	G♭	G	G♯	A♭	A
	1		2	3		4

| | 2 | 3 | 4 | 5 |

A STUDY using all the notes in the Second Position

1 Exercise on G string

Finger: 1 4 3 2 1 2 3 4

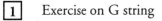

2 Exercise on D string

1 2 3 2 3 4 2 1

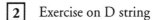

3 Exercise on A string

Finger: 4 1 2 3 4 3 2 1

4 Exercise on E string

4 2 1 2 4 3 1 3 4

5 Exercise on all four strings

String:	G	A	D	G	D	A
Finger:	4 2	3	4 2	3 4 1	2 3	4 1

A	E	A	D	A
2 3	4 1	2 3 4 2	3 4	3 4	2

Second Position

In these scales, be aware of the notes you are playing. Do not just learn the scale fingering.

This will prepare you for the following studies and chart excerpts.

BASIC STUDIES
"G" Major Scale

"C" Major Scale

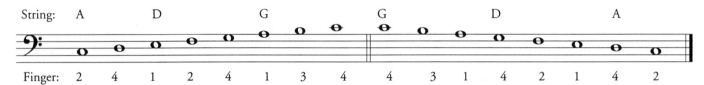

Two Studies

1
Playing in Second Position using "G" and "C" scale fingering

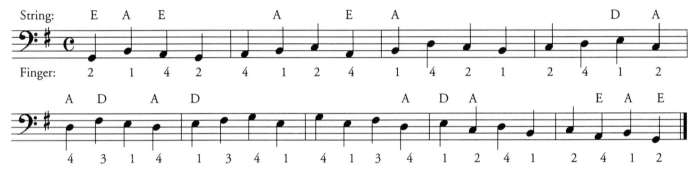

2

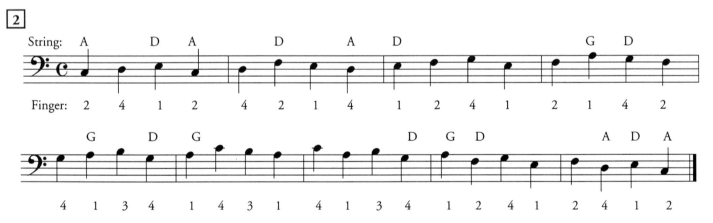

Note Review for 2nd Position

20

Playing in Second Position

Look to Note Review: For aid in locating notes (if necessary)
Look to Rhythm Studies: For aid in counting syncopation, ties, rests, etc. (if necessary)

CHART EXCERPTS

Learn the notes in these Blues Scales. They are the notes used in chart #4

CHART EXCERPTS
Using the 1st and 2nd Positions

① = 1st position, ② = 2nd position. Do not shift hand until the next position marking appears.

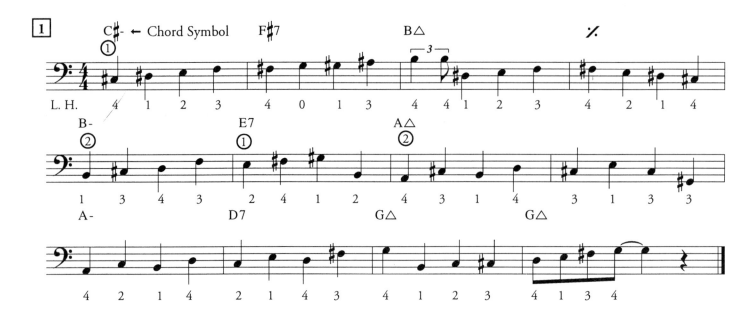

Observe the STACCATO (·) marks as they are very important to achieve the desired effect of the rhythm pattern

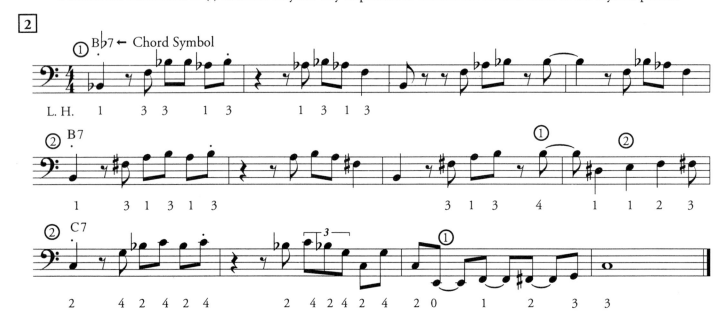

Scales and Arpeggios (Chords) in Second Position

(**x** = Pivot out of position momentarily, then back to position)

HOW TO PRACTICE: SAY and PLAY scales and arpeggios ascending and descending, as this will develop not only technical skills and note reading ability but the knowledge of the THEORY so necessary for interpreting chord symbols correctly. Begin now! Studying the Major scale chart in the "Theory for Bassist" section. Memorize the 12 Major scales, know their letter names and scale degrees. In jazz and other types of music the Major scale is used as a foundation from which we can build other scales and extract their respective chords. In these fifteen most commonly used and essential scales and the chords they generate, the scale degrees are given. ② = 2nd position, ③ = 3rd position.

SAY - PLAY - LISTEN - MEMORIZE

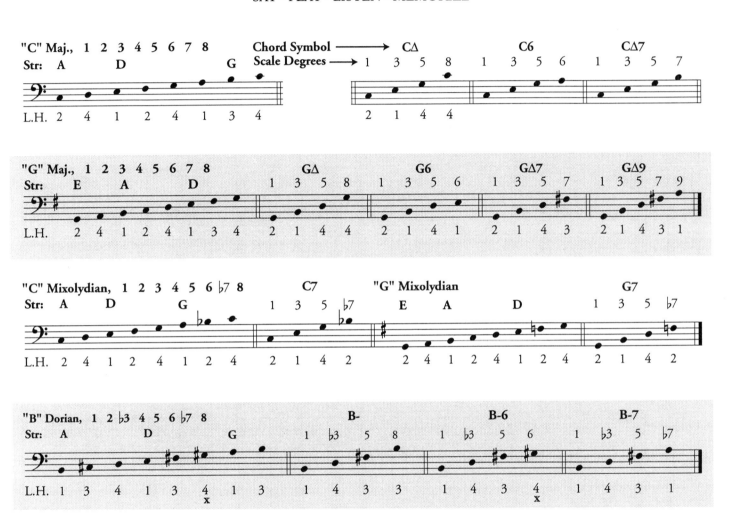

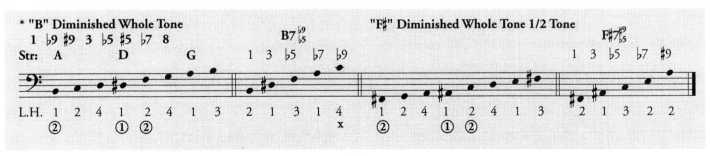

23

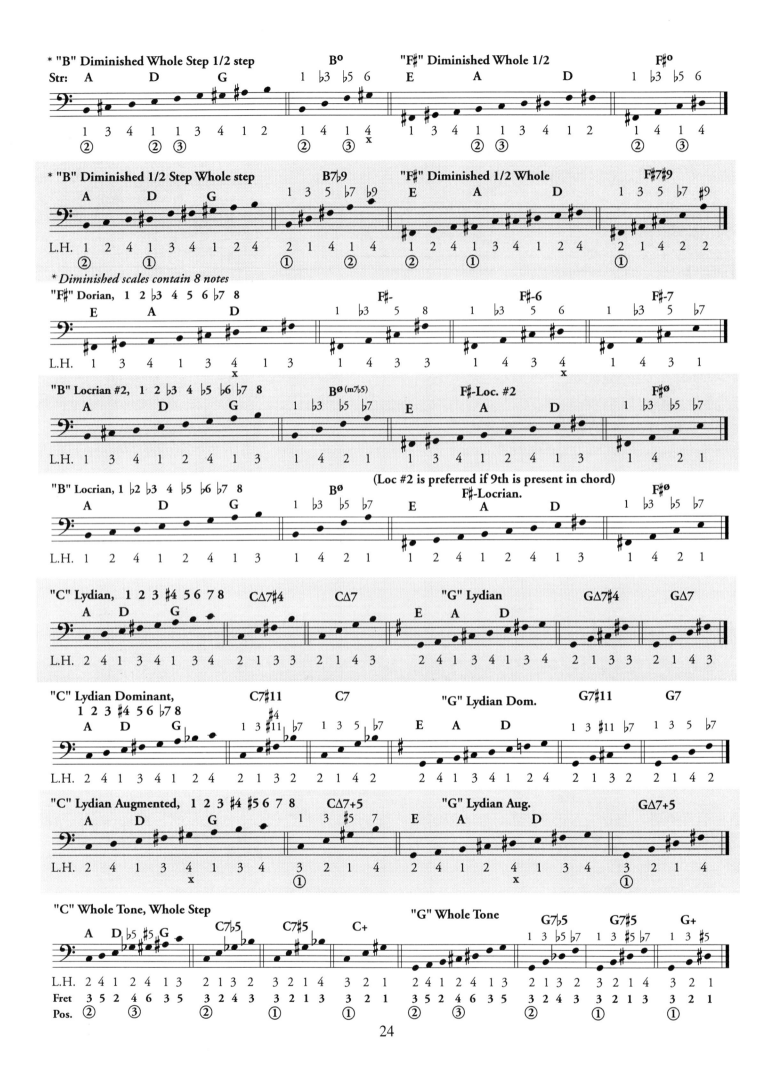

24

Second Position
Accelerated Fingerboard Study
Two Octave Scales and Arpeggios
MEMORIZE this page

"G" Major Scale: used with major type chords, G△, G6, G△7, G△9.

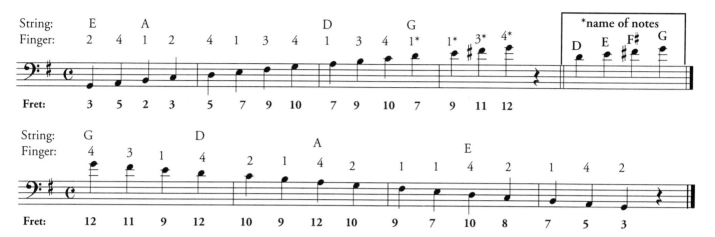

"G" Major Arpeggio: chordal function, the same as the major scale, except for the major 7th. The 7th would clash with the 1.

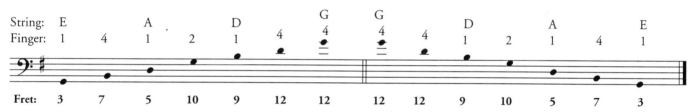

"B" Diminished Whole Tone Scale (Super Locrian): used with altered dominant chords, B7+9, B7♭9, B7 ♭9/♯5, B7 ♯9/♯5, B7 ♭9/♭5, B7 ♯9/♭5. It also sounds great over a plain dominant 7th (B7).

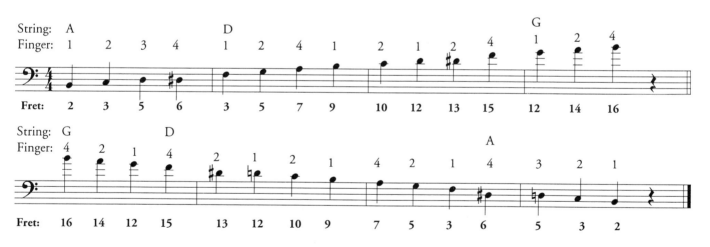

Super Locrian Arpeggio: this arpeggio is to be used with a B7 ♭9/♯5 chord.

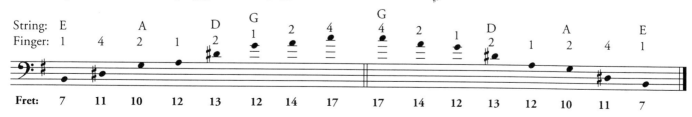

Second Position
Accelerated Fingerboard Study
Positions and Syncopated Rhythm Studies

An accelerated study, up the fingerboard from third to ninth position. Take advantage of these (Latin figures) charts. They are helpful in learning location of notes up the fingerboard.

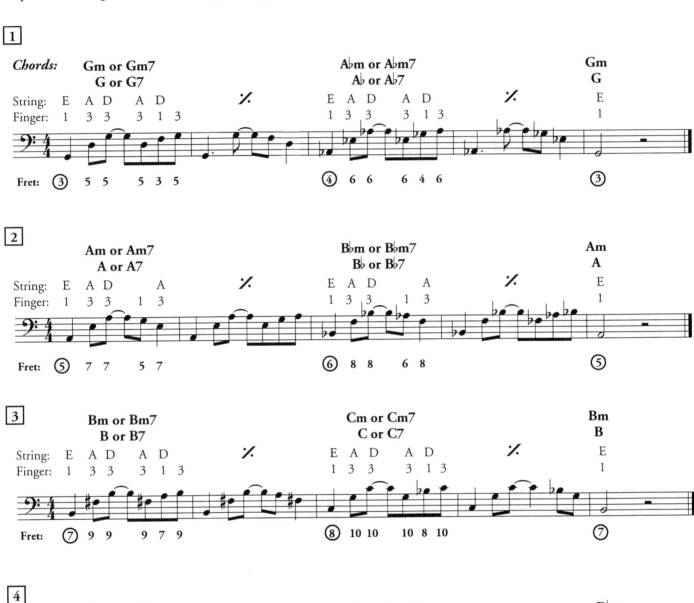

Third Position

Notes, frets, and fingerings for third position on all four strings

On the "G" string

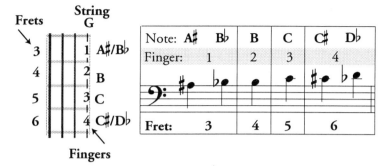

Note:	A♯	B♭	B	C	C♯	D♭
Finger:	1		2	3	4	
Fret:	3		4	5	6	

On the "D" string

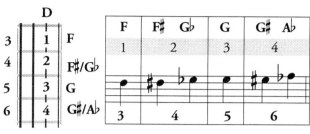

	F	F♯	G♭	G	G♯	A♭
	1	2		3	4	
	3	4		5	6	

On the "A" string

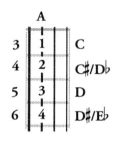
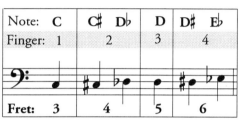

Note:	C	C♯	D♭	D	D♯	E♭
Finger:	1	2		3	4	
Fret:	3	4		5	6	

On the "E" string

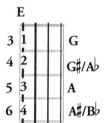

	G	G♯	A♭	A	A♯	B♭
	1	2		3	4	
	3	4		5	6	

A STUDY using all the notes in the Third Position

1 Exercise on G string

Finger: 1 3   4 3   1 4   2 1

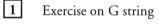

2 Exercise on D string

3 4   1 2   4 2   1

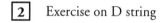

3 Exercise on A string

Finger: 1 4   2 4   3 2   1

4 Exercise on E string

4 2   3 1   2 3   4 1

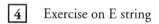

5 Exercise on all four strings

String: E A   D   G   E A   E
Finger: 2 4   2 4   4 3 2 1   4 1   2 2 1 4   2

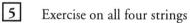
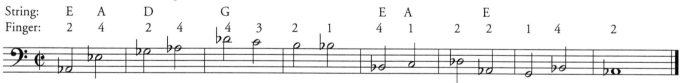

6

String: A D   G   D   *   A E   A
Finger: 2 1   4 1   4 2 1 4   2 1   4 2 4 1   2

* "E♯" is the same as "F"

27

Third Position

In these scales, be aware of the notes you are playing.

This will prepare you for the following studies and chart excerpts.

BASIC STUDIES
"A♭" Major Scale

"D♭" Major Scale

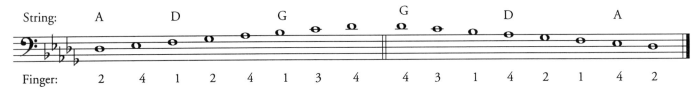

Two Studies

Playing in Third Position using "A♭" and "D♭" scale fingering

1

2

Note Review for 3rd Position

28

Playing in Third Position

Look to Note Review: For aid in locating notes (if necessary)

Look to Rhythm Studies: For aid in counting syncopation, ties, rests, etc. (if necessary)

CHART EXCERPTS

Learn the notes in these Blues Scales. They are the notes used in chart #4

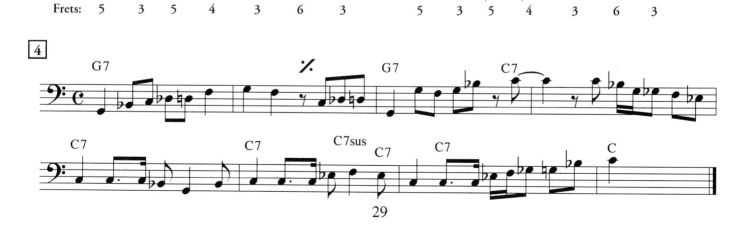

Scales and Arpeggios (Chords) in Third Position

For practice procedures see Scales and Arpeggios Studies in Second Position

(Loc #2 is preferred if 9th is present in chord)

Third Position
Accelerated Fingerboard Study
Two Octave Scales and Arpeggios

MEMORIZE this page

"A♭" Major Scale: used with major type chords, Ab△, Ab6, Ab△7, Ab△9, Ab9 $\frac{9}{6}$

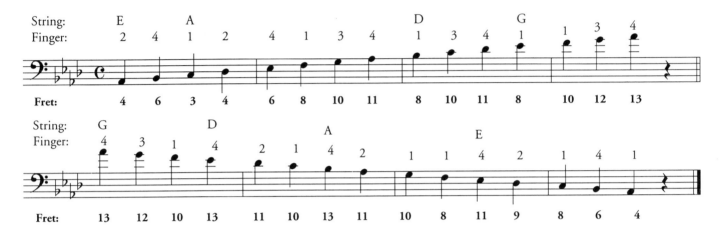

"A♭" Major Arpeggio: chordal function, the same as the major scale.

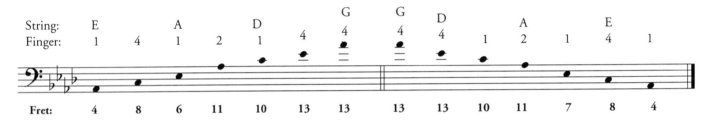

"G" Harmonic Minor Scale: used with Gm, G-(m)7, G-△7. Not good for minor 6th chords.

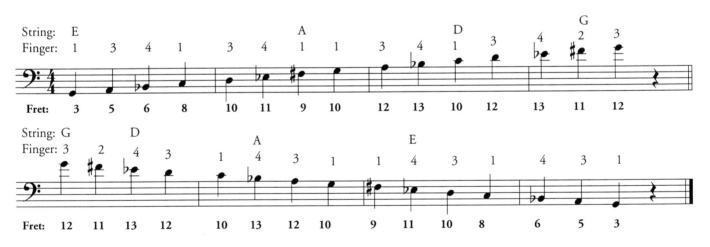

"G" Minor Major 7th Arpeggio: chordal function the same as the harmonic minor scale.

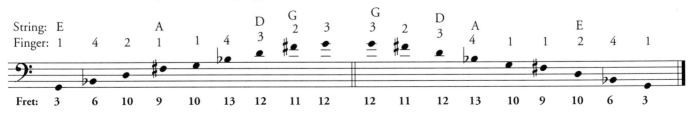

Third Position
Accelerated Studies
Positions and Syncopated Rhythm Studies

Two charts that force hand shifts. Practice slowly. No. 1 contains REAL information on *How and When to Shift Positions.*

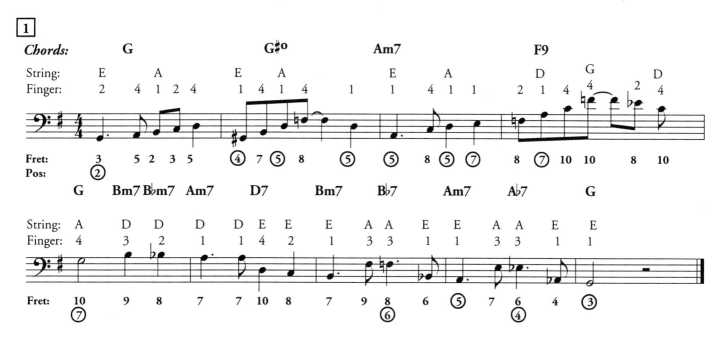

* NO. 2 has, in the last line second measure, the long jump "G" to "G". In this case it is best accomplished by a first to fourth finger shift.

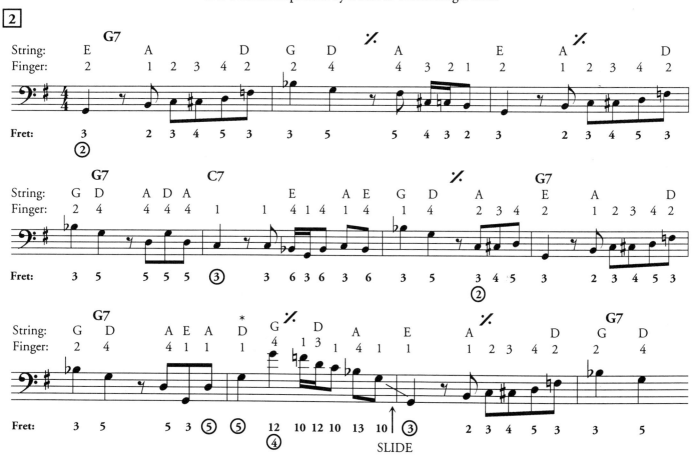

Fourth Position

Notes, frets, and fingerings for fourth position on all four strings

On the "G" string

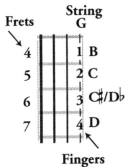

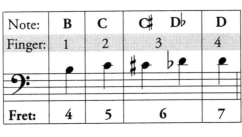

On the "D" string

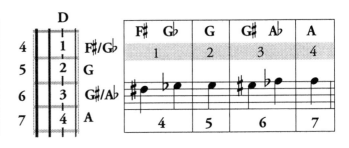

On the "A" string

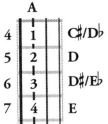

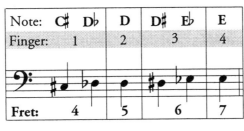

On the "E" string

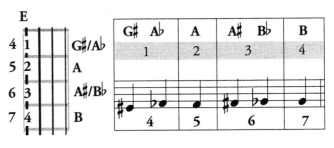

1   Exercise on G string

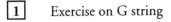

2   Exercise on D string

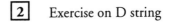

3   Exercise on A string

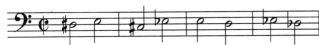

4   Exercise on E string

5   Exercise on all four strings

6

Fourth Position

In these scales, be aware of the notes you are playing.

This will prepare you for the following studies and chart excerpts.

BASIC STUDIES
"A" Major Scale

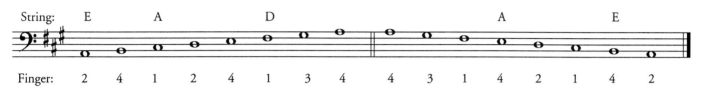

"D" Major Scale

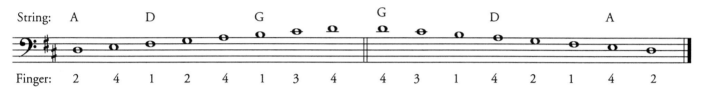

Two Studies
Playing in Fourth Position using "A" and "D" scale fingering

1

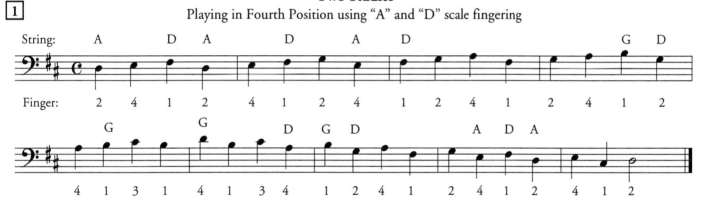

2

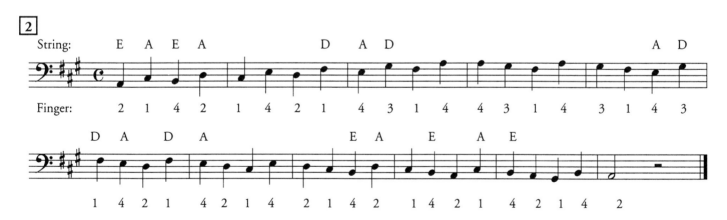

Note Review for 4th Position

35

Playing in Fourth Position

Look to Note Review: For aid in locating notes (if necessary)

Look to Rhythm Studies: For aid in counting syncopation, ties, rests, etc. (if necessary)

CHART EXCERPTS

Learn the notes in these Blues Scales. They are the notes used in chart #4

Scales and Arpeggios (Chords) in Fourth Position

For practice procedures see Scales and Arpeggios Studies in Second Position

Scales and Arpeggios (Chords) in Fourth Position

For practice procedures see Scales and Arpeggios Studies in Second Position

Fourth Position
Accelerated Fingerboard Study
Two Octave Scales and Arpeggios
MEMORIZE this page

"A" Major Scale: used with major type chords, AΔ, A6, AΔ7, AΔ9, A9$\frac{9}{6}$

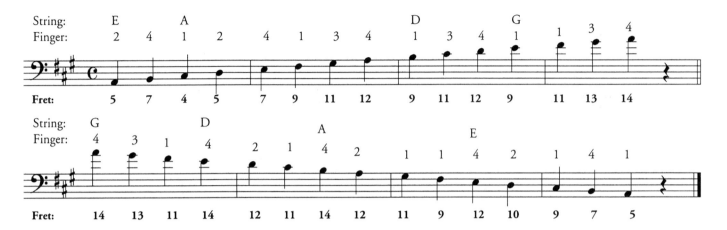

"A" Major Arpeggio: chordal function, the same as the major scale.

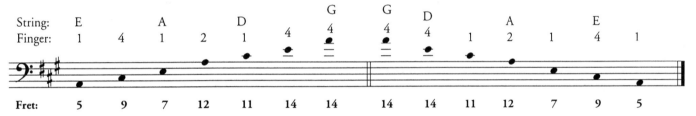

"A" Whole Tone Scale: normally used with dominant 7th chords which has either a raised or lowered 5th or both (A7♯5♭5). It can also be used for augmented chords (A+, A7♯5).

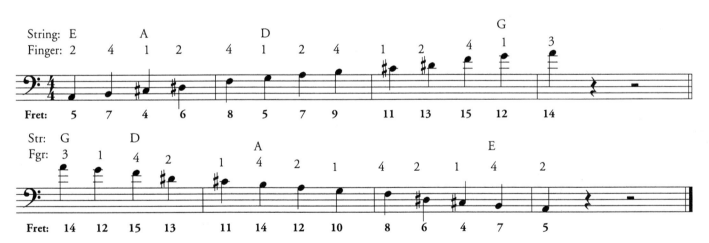

"A" Augmented Arpeggio (Aug. Triads) function the same as whole tone scale over chords.

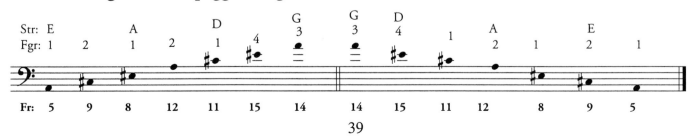

Fourth Position
Chart Excerpts
Positions and Syncopated Rhythm Studies
An accelerated study, up the fingerboard from third to tenth position.

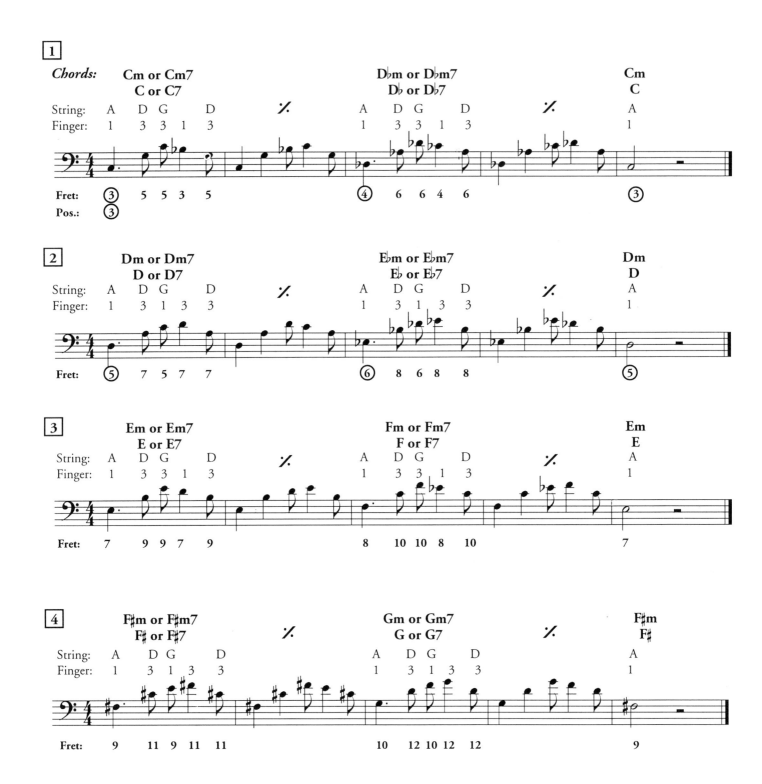

Fifth Position

Notes, frets, and fingerings for fifth position on all four strings

On the "G" string

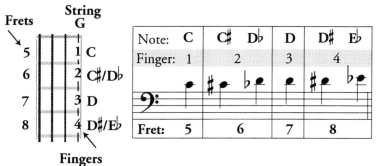

On the "D" string

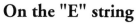
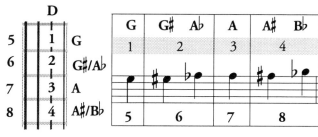

On the "A" string

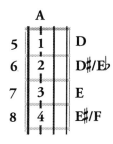

On the "E" string

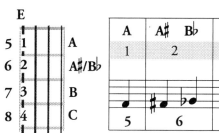

1   Exercise on G string

2   Exercise on D string

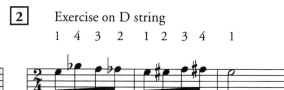

3   Exercise on A string

4   Exercise on E string

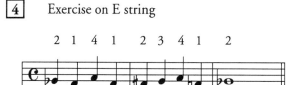

5   Exercise on all four strings

6

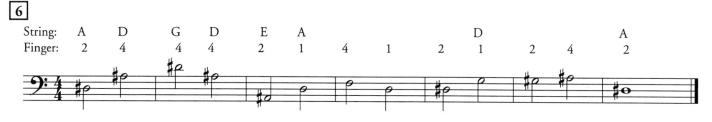

Fifth Position

In these scales, be aware of the notes you are playing.

This will prepare you for the following studies and chart excerpts.

BASIC STUDIES

"E♭" Major Scale

"B♭" Major Scale

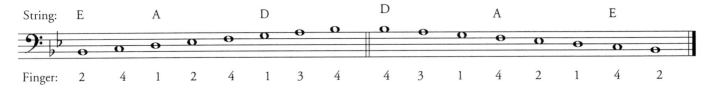

Two Studies
Playing in Fourth Position using "E♭" and "B♭" scale fingering

 1

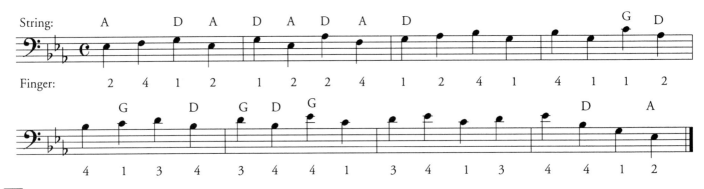

2

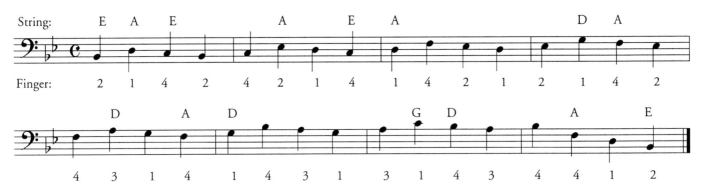

Playing in Fifth Position
Note Review for 5th Position

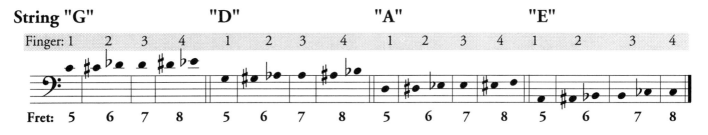

Look to Note Review: For aid in locating notes (if necessary)

Look to Rhythm Studies: For aid in counting syncopation, ties, rests, etc. (if necessary)

CHART EXCERPTS

Soli = in jazz bands and combos, the bass player quite often plays unison passages with the horns.

Fifth Position Studies

Extension Fingerings: Extend or pivot out of position momentarily. Chart studies $\boxed{1}$ and $\boxed{2}$ use extension fingerings, demonstrating the vast range of 5th position when using the extensions. A GREAT AID when reading music. $\boxed{3}$ plays from first ① to ⑥ position.

Note Review for 5th Position with Extension (x) Fingerings

Look to Note Review: For aid in locating notes (if necessary)

Look to Rhythm Studies: For aid in counting syncopation, ties, rests, etc. (if necessary)

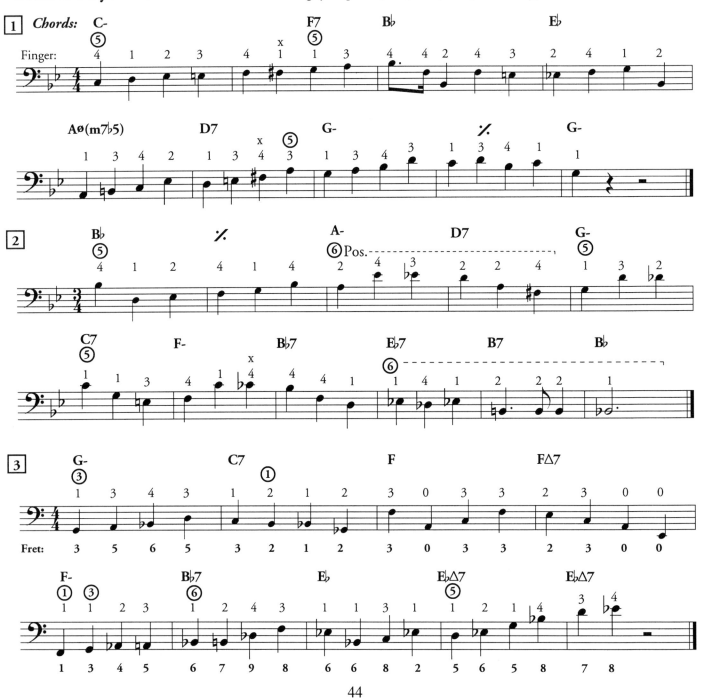

44

Scales and Arpeggios (Chords) in Fifth Position

For practice procedures see Scales and Arpeggios Studies in Second Position

Scales and Arpeggios (Chords) in Fifth Position

For practice procedures see Scales and Arpeggios Studies in Second Position

Fifth Position
Accelerated Fingerboard Study
Two Octave Scales and Arpeggios
MEMORIZE this page

"B♭" Major Scale: used with major type chords, B♭Δ, B♭6, B♭Δ7, B♭Δ9

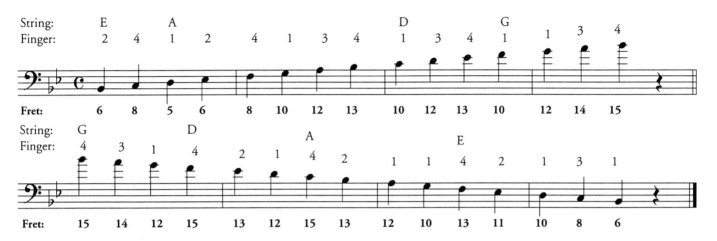

"B♭" Major Arpeggio: chordal function, the same as the major scale except for the Major 7th. The 7th would clash with the 1(one) or the 8th.

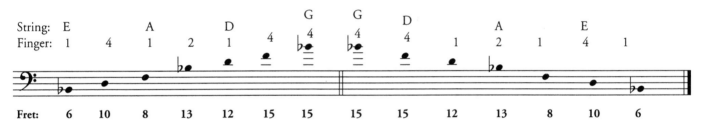

"B♭" Mixolydian Scale: used with dominant 7th chords, B♭7.

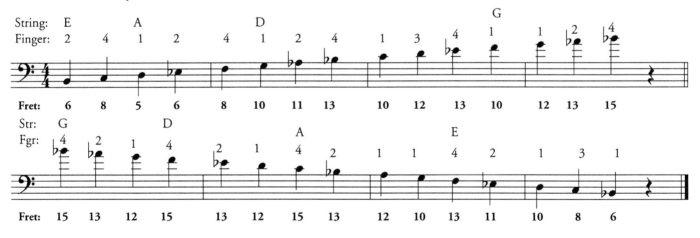

"B♭" Dominant 7th Arpeggio: chordal function the same as the Mixolydian scale.

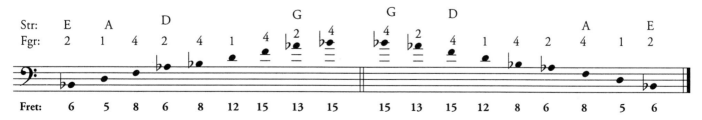

Sixth Position

Notes, frets, and fingerings for sixth position on all four strings

On the "G" string

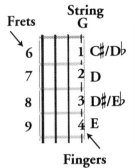

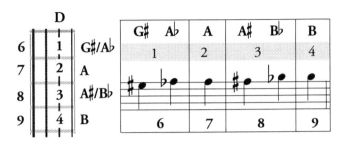

Note:	C♯	D♭	D	D♯	E♭	E
Finger:	1		2	3		4
Fret:	6		7	8		9

On the "D" string

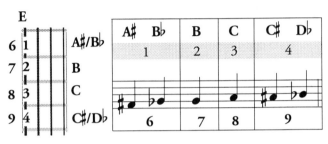

Note:	G♯	A♭	A	A♯	B♭	B
Finger:	1		2	3		4
Fret:	6		7	8		9

On the "A" string

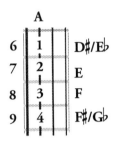

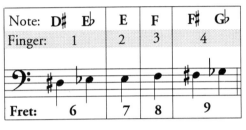

Note:	D♯	E♭	E	F	F♯	G♭
Finger:	1		2	3	4	
Fret:	6		7	8	9	

On the "E" string

Note:	A♯	B♭	B	C	C♯	D♭
Finger:	1		2	3	4	
Fret:	6		7	8	9	

---

1 Exercise on G string

Finger: 1 2 3 2 4 1 3 1

2 Exercise on D string

4 1 3 4 4 2 3 1

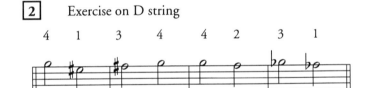

3 Exercise on A string

Finger: 4 3 1 3 4 1 3 1 4 1

4 Exercise on E string

1 4 3 1 2 1 4 1

5 Exercise on all four strings

String: E   A   D   A   D   G
Finger: 1 3 4 1 3 4 2 3   3   3   1 3 4 1 3 4* 2 3

6

String: E   A   D   G   D   A E A
Finger: 2   1   4   1   2 1   4 1 3   4 1 4 1 2 1 1 1   2

*"C♭" is the same as "B"

48

Sixth Position

In these scales, be aware of the notes you are playing.

This will prepare you for the following studies and chart excerpts.

BASIC STUDIES

"E" Major Scale

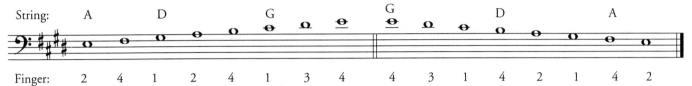

"B" Major Scale

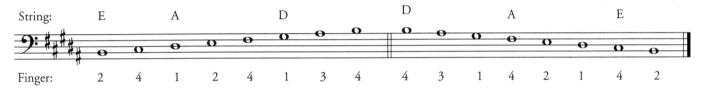

Two Studies

1 Playing in sixth Position using "E" and "B" scale fingering

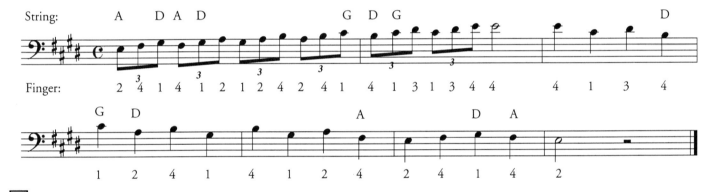

2

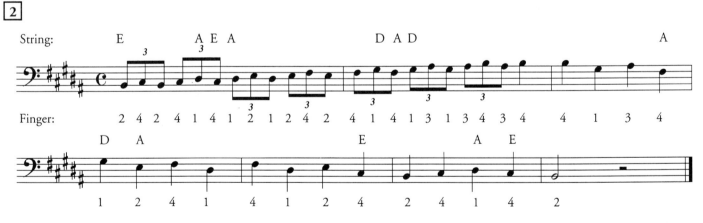

Sixth Position

Studies ☐1 and ☐2 cover all positions studied so far, ① thru ⑥.   Position number will be marked ⑥, finger 2, i.e. 6th position 2nd finger. IF NECESSARY: refer to "Fingerboard Positions and Note Location Chart to the 12th Fret" for assistance in locating the proper fret and string for the given position.

CHART EXCERPTS 6TH POSITION ONLY

Scales and Arpeggios (Chords) in Sixth Position

For practice procedures see Scales and Arpeggios Studies in Second Position

51

Scales and Arpeggios (Chords) in Sixth Position

For practice procedures see Scales and Arpeggios Studies in Second Position

52

Sixth Position
Accelerated Fingerboard Study
Two Octave Scales and Arpeggios
MEMORIZE this page

"B" Major Scale: used with major type chords, BΔ, B6, BΔ7, BΔ9

"B" Major Arpeggio: chordal function is the same as the major scale except for the Major 7th. The 7th would clash with the 1 (one) or the 8th.

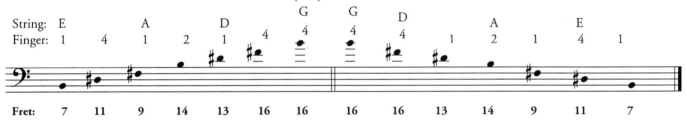

"B♭" Ascending Melodic Minor Scale: used with minor type chords, C-, C-6, C-Δ7; also referred to as the "Jazz Melodic Minor Scale".

"B♭" Minor Arpeggio: chordal function is the same as the ascending melodic minor scale.

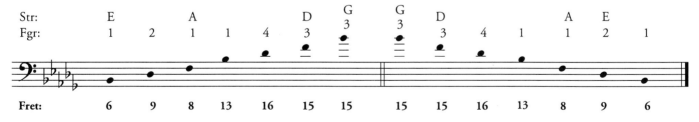

Seventh Position

Notes, frets, and fingerings for seventh position on all four strings

On the "G" string

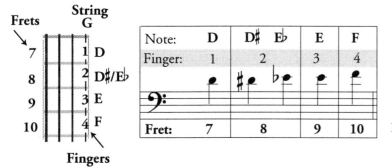

On the "D" string

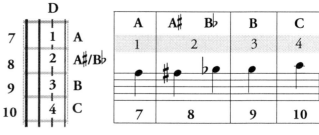

On the "A" string

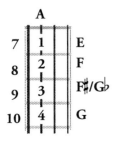

On the "E" string

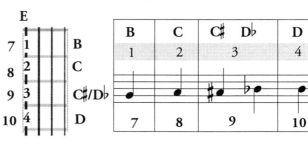

1 Exercise on G string

2 Exercise on D string

3 Exercise on A string

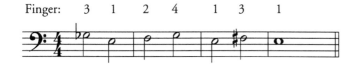

4 Exercise on E string

5 Exercise on all four strings

6

54

Seventh Position

In these scales, be aware of the notes you are playing.

This will prepare you for the following studies and chart excerpts.

BASIC STUDIES

"F" Major Scale

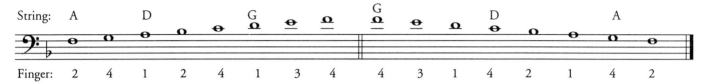

String:	A		D			G			G				D		A
Finger:	2	4	1	2	4	1	3	4	4	3	1	4	2	1	4	2

"C" Major Scale

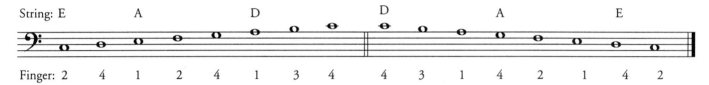

String:	E		A			D			D			A			E
Finger:	2	4	1	2	4	1	3	4	4	3	1	4	2	1	4	2

Two Studies
Playing in Seventh Position

1

String:	G			D	G	D				A	D	A				E
Finger:	4	1	3	4	1	2	4	1	2	4	1	2	4	1	2	4

	A	E		A		D				G			D		A
	1	2	4	1	2	1	2	3	4	1	3	4	1	4	2

2

String:	E	A			D				G				D		
Finger:	2	1	2	3	4	1	2	3	4	1	2	3	4	2	4	3

	D		A			E			A		D		
	2	4	2	3	4	2	4	1	2	1	4	1	4

Note Review for 7th Position

String "G"   **"D"**   **"A"**   **"E"**

Finger:	1	2	3	4	1	2	3	4	1	2	3	4	1	2	3	4

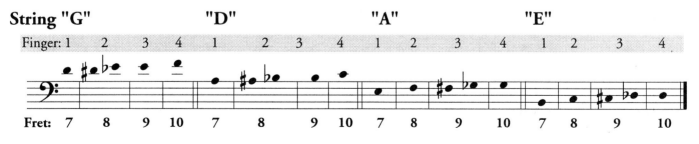

Fret:	7	8	9	10	7	8	9	10	7	8	9	10	7	8	9	10

Playing in Seventh Position

CHART EXCERPTS

Playing from ⑦ to ① position

Scales and Arpeggios (Chords) in Seventh Position

For practice procedures see Scales and Arpeggios Studies in Second Position

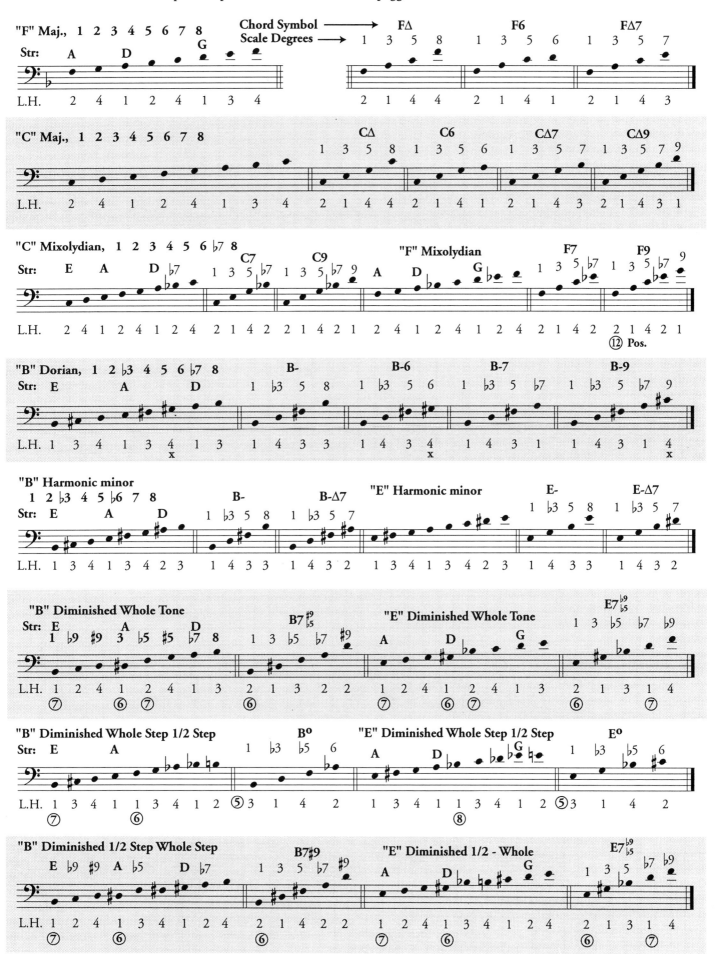

57

Scales and Arpeggios (Chords) in Seventh Position

For practice procedures see Scales and Arpeggios Studies in Second Position

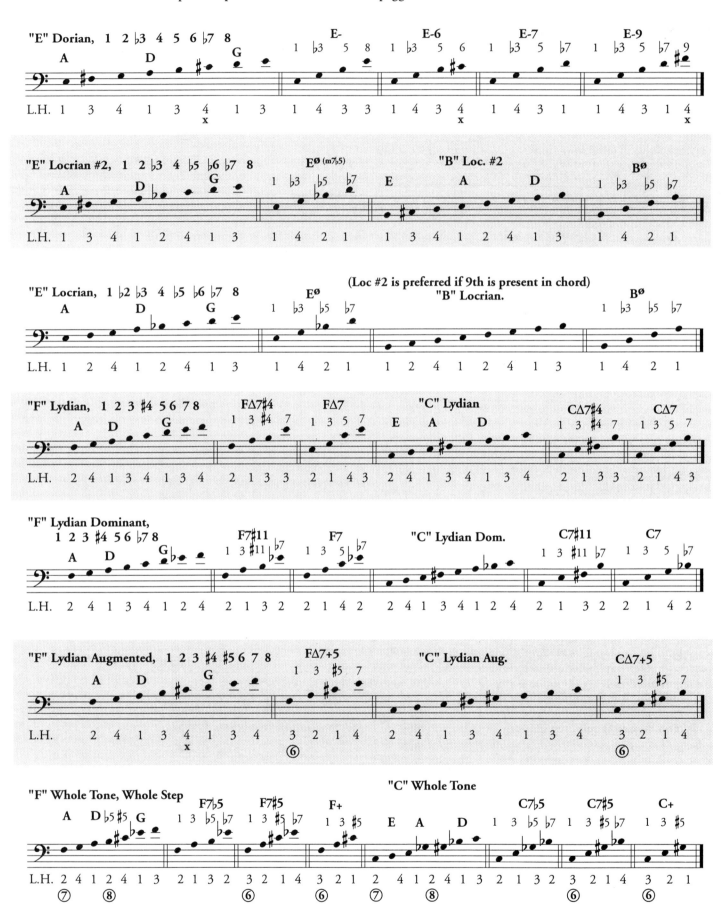

Seventh Position
Accelerated Fingerboard Study
Two Octave Scales and Arpeggios

MEMORIZE this page

"C" Major Scale: used with major type chords, C, C6, CΔ7, CΔ9

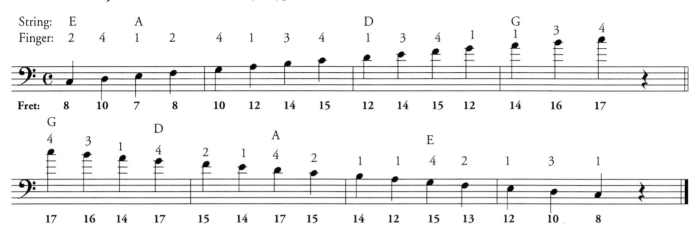

"C" Major Arpeggio: chordal function is the same as the major scale except for the Major 7th. The 7th would clash with the 1 (one) or the 8th.

"B" Locrian #2 Scale: used with half diminished chords (symbol: ø) is actually a minor 7 chord with a flat 5 (♭5).

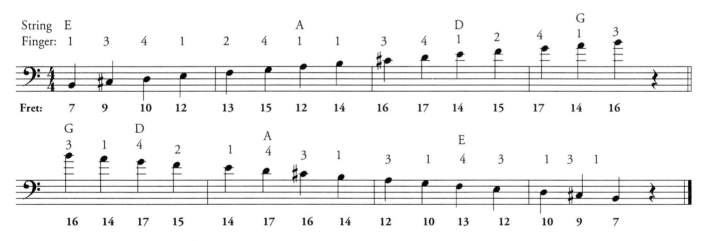

"B" Half Diminished (ø) Arpeggio: chordal function is the same as the Locrian #2.

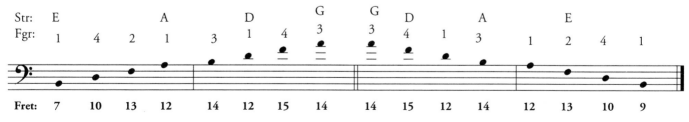

Eighth Position

Notes, frets, and fingerings for eighth position on all four strings

On the "G" string

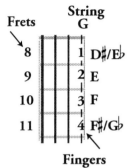

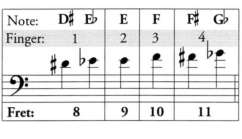

Note:	D♯ E♭	E	F	F♯ G♭
Finger:	1	2	3	4
Fret:	8	9	10	11

On the "D" string

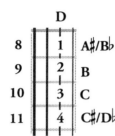

Note:	A♯ B♭	B	C	C♯ D♭
	1	2	3	4
Fret:	8	9	10	11

On the "A" string

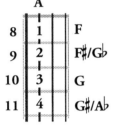

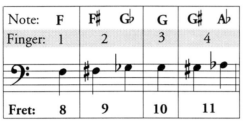

Note:	F	F♯ G♭	G	G♯ A♭
Finger:	1	2	3	4
Fret:	8	9	10	11

On the "E" string

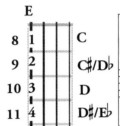

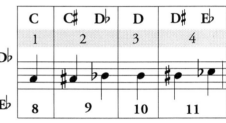

Note:	C	C♯ D♭	D	D♯ E♭
	1	2	3	4
Fret:	8	9	10	11

1 Exercise on G string

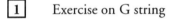

2 Exercise on D string

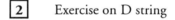

3 Exercise on A string

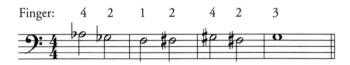

4 Exercise on E string

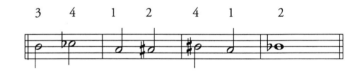

5 Exercise on all four strings

6

60

Eighth Position

In these scales, be aware of the notes you are playing.

This will prepare you for the following studies and chart excerpts.

BASIC STUDIES

"F♯" Major Scale

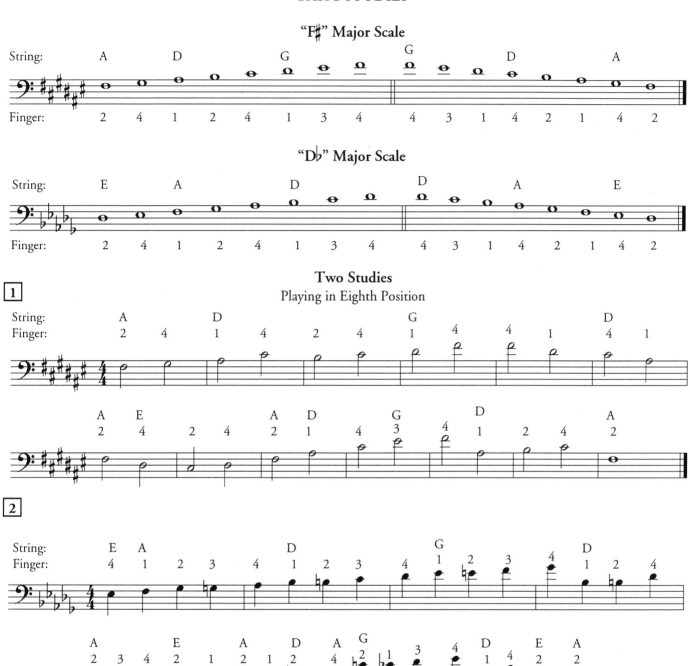

"D♭" Major Scale

Two Studies
Playing in Eighth Position

Eighth Position

CHART EXCERPTS
Playing from first to eighth position

"G♭" Major Scale

Learn the notes in these blues scales — they are the notes used in chart #2

E Blues Scale   **B Blues Scale**

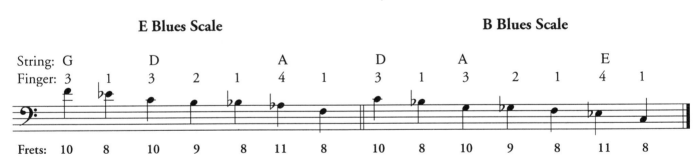

* Slide

Scales and Arpeggios (Chords) in Eighth Position

For practice procedures see Scales and Arpeggios Studies in Second Position

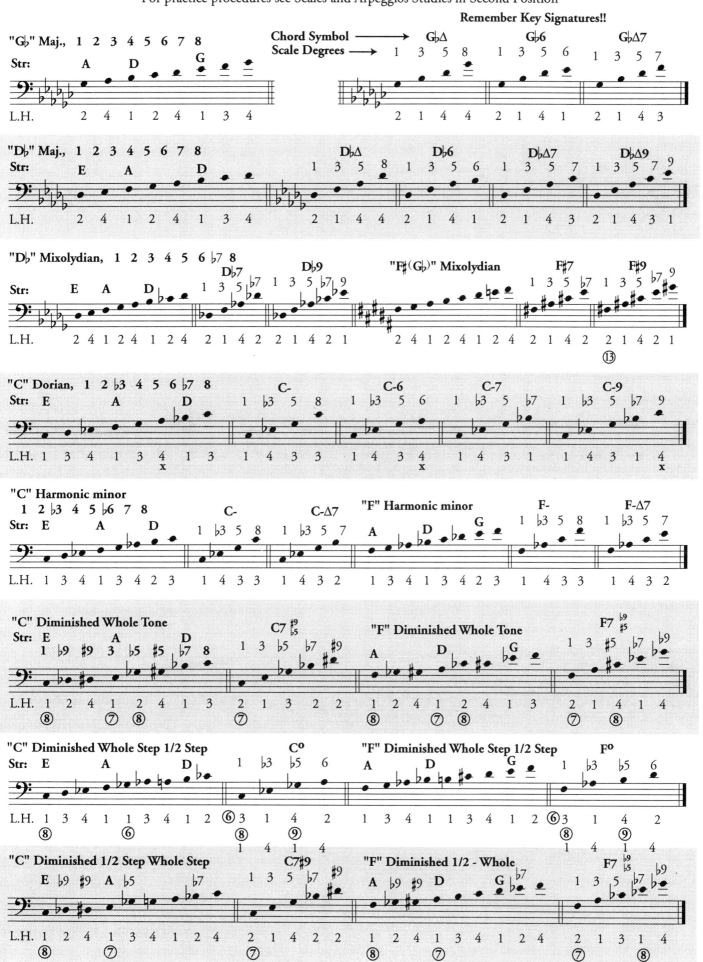

63

Scales and Arpeggios (Chords) in Eighth Position

For practice procedures see Scales and Arpeggios Studies in Second Position

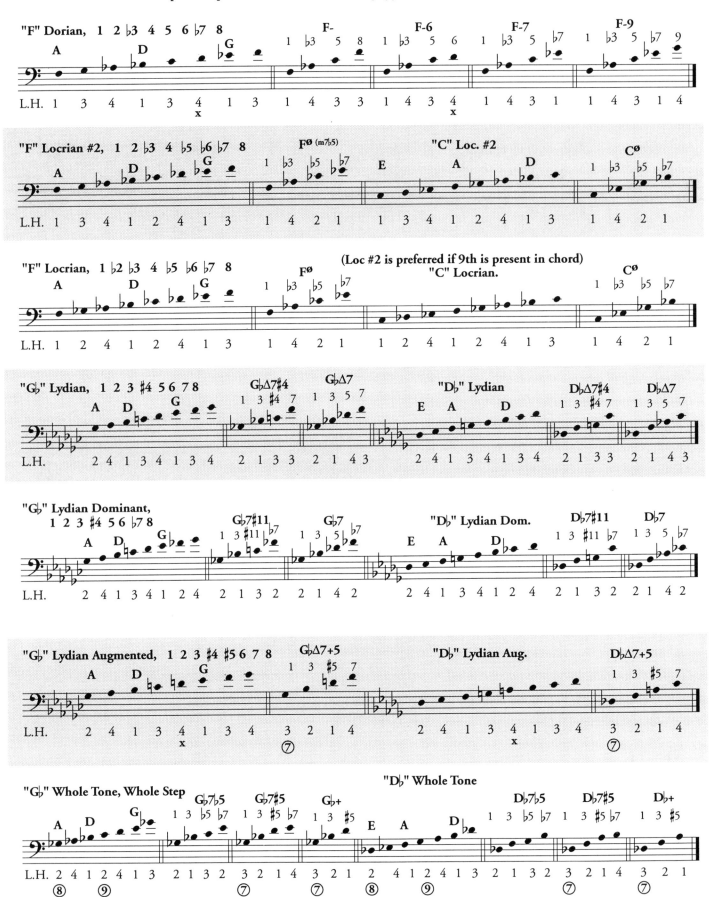

Eighth Position
Two Octave Scale Fingering
Accelerated Studies

"D♭" Major Scale: from eighth to fifteenth position.

"D♭" Major Scale: from ninth to fifteenth position.

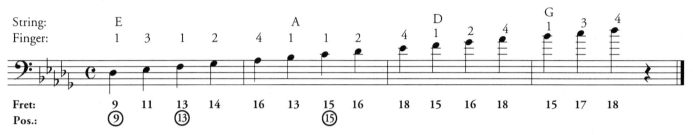

A Shifting Study in "D♭" Major

playing from ninth to fifteenth position.

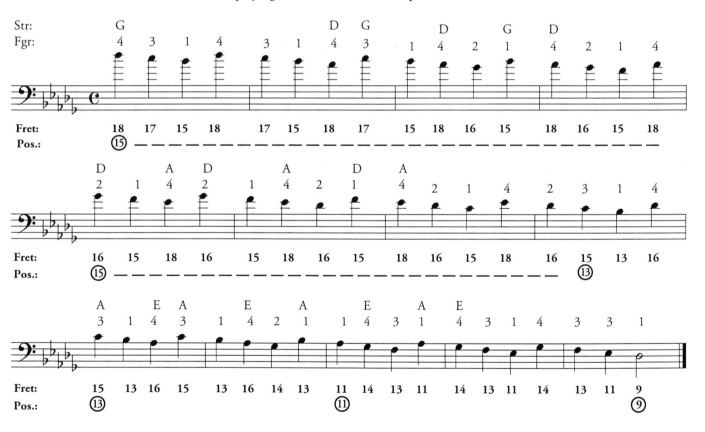

Ninth Position

Notes, frets, and fingerings for ninth position on all four strings

On the "G" string

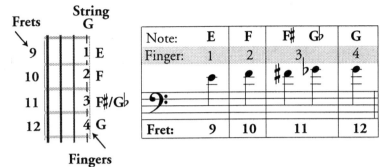

Note:	E	F	F#	Gb	G
Finger:	1	2	3		4
Fret:	9	10	11		12

On the "D" string

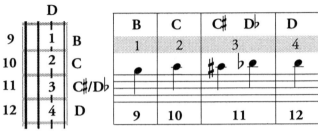

Note:	B	C	C#	Db	D
Finger:	1	2	3		4
Fret:	9	10	11		12

On the "A" string

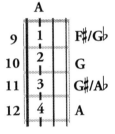

Note:	F#	Gb	G	G#	Ab	A
Finger:	1		2	3		4
Fret:	9		10	11		12

On the "E" string

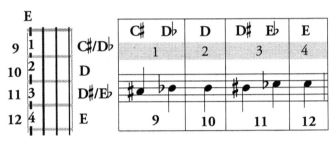

Note:	C#	Db	D	D#	Eb	E
Finger:	1		2	3		4
Fret:	9		10	11		12

1 Exercise on G string

2 Exercise on D string

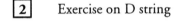

3 Exercise on A string

4 Exercise on E string

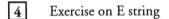

5 Exercise on all four strings

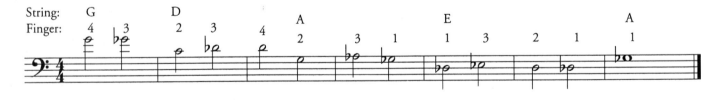

6

Ninth Position

In these scales, be aware of the notes you are playing.

This will prepare you for the following studies and chart excerpts.

BASIC STUDIES

"G" Major Scale

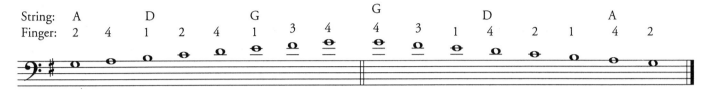

"D" Major Scale

Two Studies

1
Playing in Ninth Position

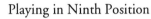

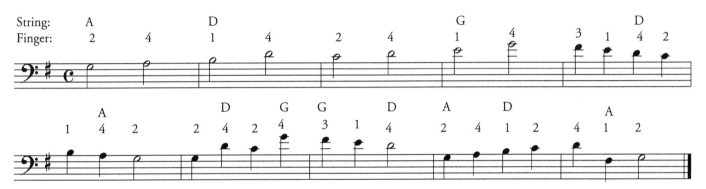

2

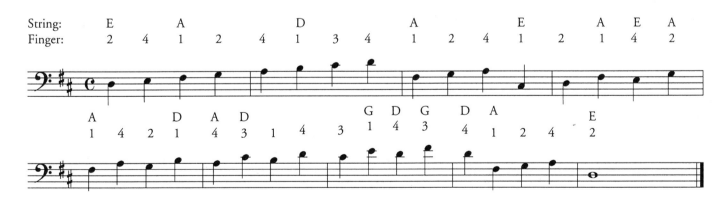

67

Ninth Position

CHART EXCERPTS

Playing from ninth to second position
and back to ninth position

Learn the notes in these blues scales — they are the notes used in chart #2

* Slide

Ninth Position

Accelerated Fingering: "D" Major Scale playing from the 9th to the 16th position.

Chart Excerpt: covering positions ⑤ through ⑨

"D" Major Scale
Accelerated Fingering from 9th to 16th position.

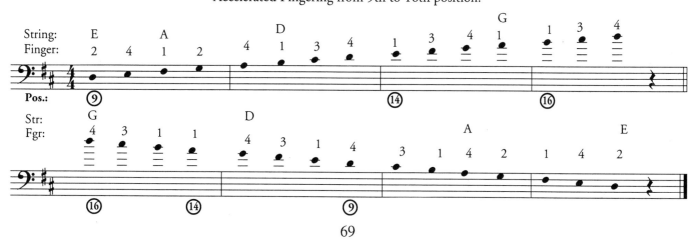

Tenth Position

Notes, frets, and fingerings for tenth position on all four strings

On the "G" string

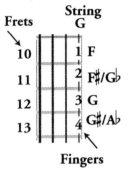
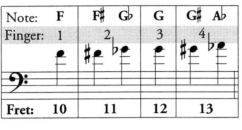

On the "D" string

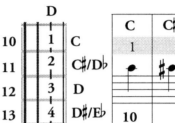

On the "A" string

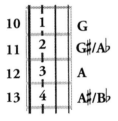

On the "E" string

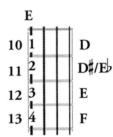

1   Exercise on G string

2   Exercise on D string

3   Exercise on A string

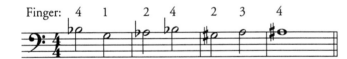

4   Exercise on E string

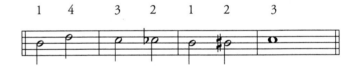

5   Exercise on all four strings

6

Tenth Position

In these scales, be aware of the notes you are playing.

This will prepare you for the following studies and chart excerpts.

BASIC STUDIES

"A♭" Major Scale

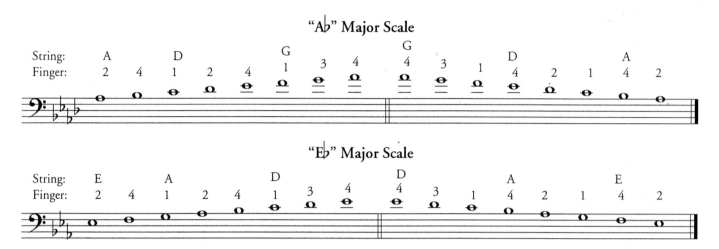

"E♭" Major Scale

Two Studies
Playing in Tenth Position

1

2

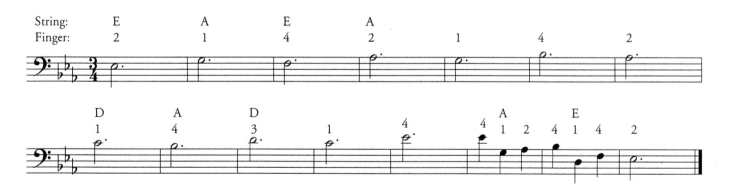

Tenth Position

CHART EXCERPTS
Playing in the tenth position

"G" Blues Scale covering positions ③ through ⑩

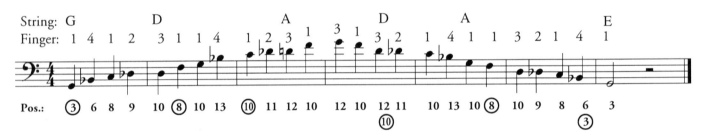

* NOTICE: when playing a dotted 8th and 16th note with a dot over the dotted 8th note, play the dotted 8th staccato, causing a 16th rest between the notes (♪ 𝄽 ♪).

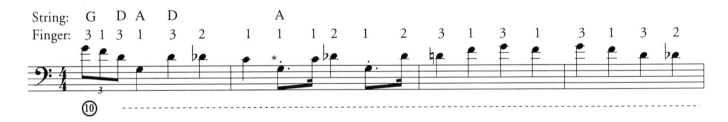

Eleventh Position

Notes, frets, and fingerings for eleventh position on all four strings

On the "G" string

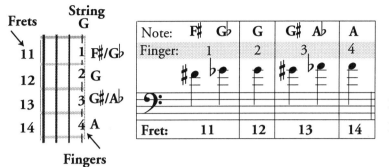

On the "D" string

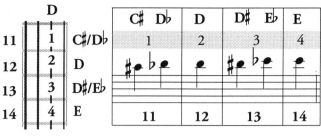

On the "A" string

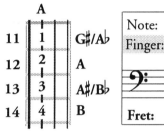
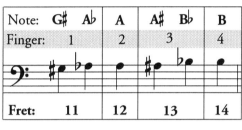

On the "E" string

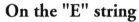

1   Exercise on G string

2   Exercise on D string

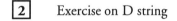

3   Exercise on A string

4   Exercise on E string

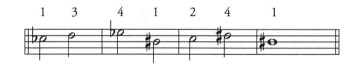

5   Exercise on all four strings

6

Eleventh Position

In these scales, be aware of the notes you are playing.

This will prepare you for the following studies and chart excerpts.

BASIC STUDIES

"A" Major Scale

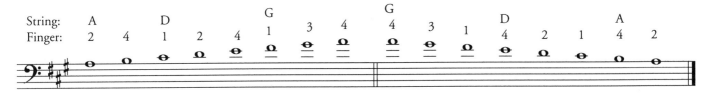

"E" Major Scale

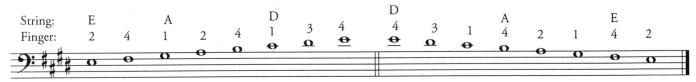

Two Studies
Playing in Eleventh Position

1

2

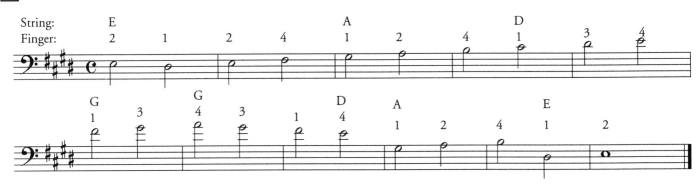

Eleventh Position

CHART EXCERPTS
Playing in the eleventh position

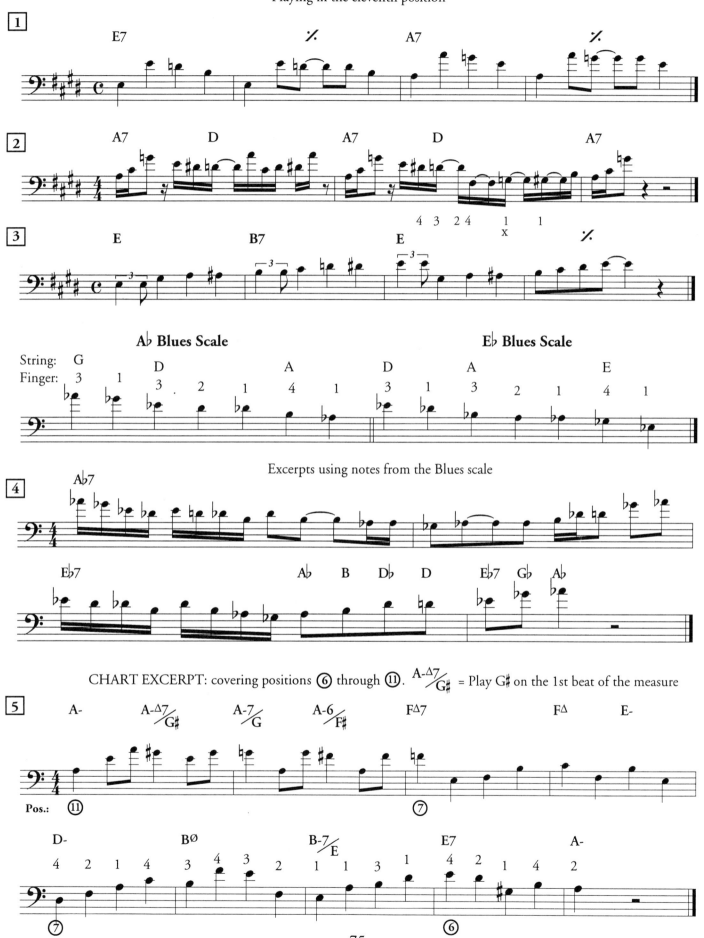

CHART EXCERPT: covering positions ⑥ through ⑪. A-Δ7/G# = Play G# on the 1st beat of the measure

Twelfth Position

Notes, frets, and fingerings for twelfth position on all four strings

On the "G" string

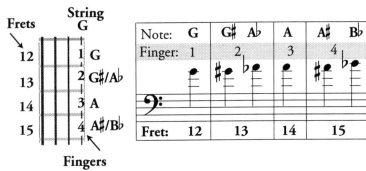

Note:	G	G# Ab	A	A# Bb
Finger:	1	2	3	4
Fret:	12	13	14	15

On the "D" string

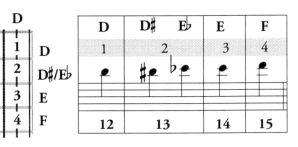

Note:	D	D# Eb	E	F
Finger:	1	2	3	4
Fret:	12	13	14	15

On the "A" string

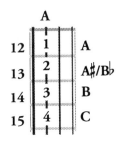

Note:	A	A# Bb	B	C
Finger:	1	2	3	4
Fret:	12	13	14	15

On the "E" string

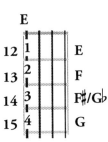

Note:	E	F	F# Gb	G
Finger:	1	2	3	4
Fret:	12	13	14	15

1 Exercise on G string

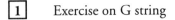

2 Exercise on D string

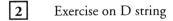

3 Exercise on A string

4 Exercise on E string

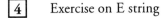

Twelfth Position

A = 12th Position Basic Studies
B = HARMONIZED, Harmonic Minor and Major Scales (Diatonic 7ths). Positions ⑤ through ⑫ MEMORIZE

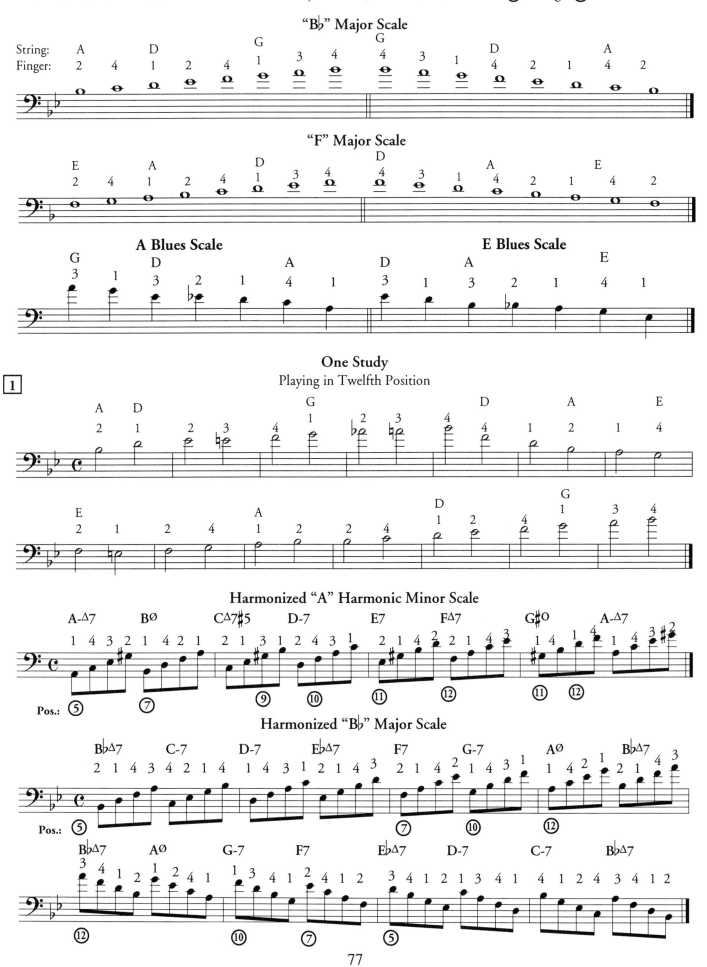

77

Thirteenth Position

Notes, frets, and fingerings for thirteenth position on all four strings

On the "G" string

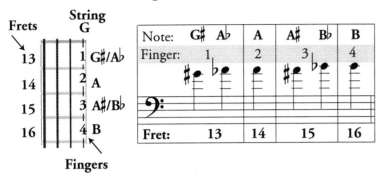

On the "D" string

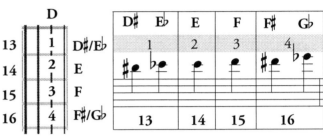

On the "A" string

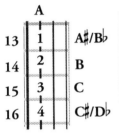
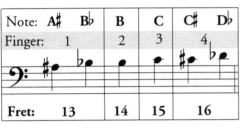

On the "E" string

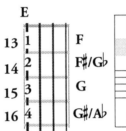
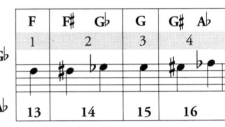

1 Exercise on G string

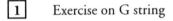

2 Exercise on D string

3 Exercise on A string

4 Exercise on E string

5 Exercise on all four strings

6

* "E♯" is the same as "F".

78

Thirteenth Position

A = 13th Position Basic Studies
B = HARMONIZED, Harmonic Minor and Major Scales (Diatonic 7ths). Positions ⑥ through ⑬, MEMORIZE

"B" Major Scale

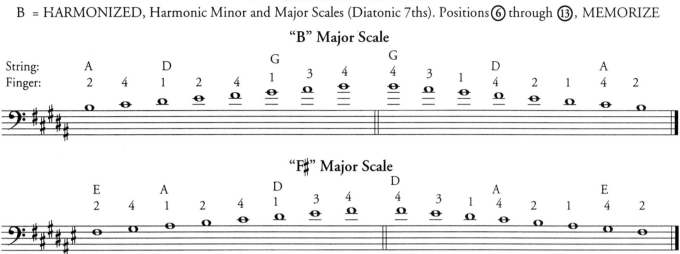

"F♯" Major Scale

B♭ Blues Scale   F Blues Scale

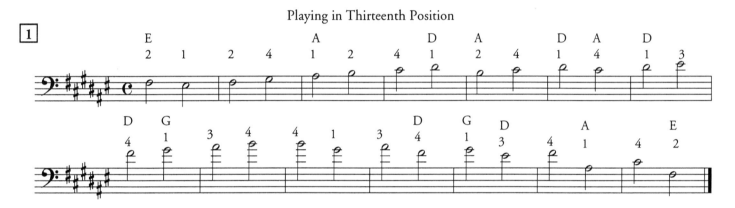

Playing in Thirteenth Position

Harmonized "B♭" Harmonic Minor Scale

Harmonized "B" Major Scale

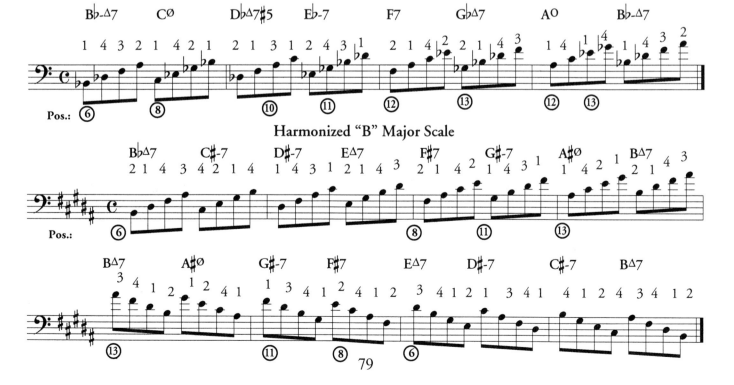

79

Fourteenth Position

Notes, frets, and fingerings for fourteenth position on all four strings

On the "G" string

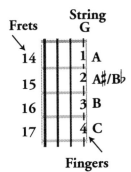

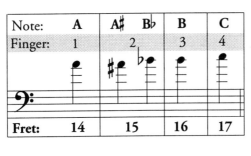

On the "D" string

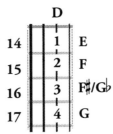

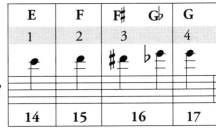

On the "A" string

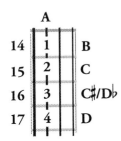

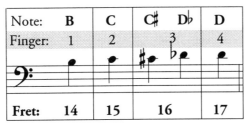

On the "E" string

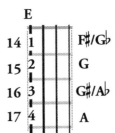

1   Exercise on G string

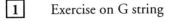

2   Exercise on D string

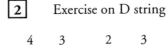

3   Exercise on A string

4   Exercise on E string

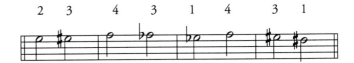

5   Exercise on all four strings

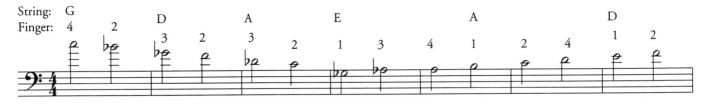

Fourteenth Position

A = 14th Position Basic Studies
B = HARMONIZED, Harmonic Minor and Major Scales (Diatonic 7ths). Positions ⑦ through ⑭, MEMORIZE

"C" Major Scale

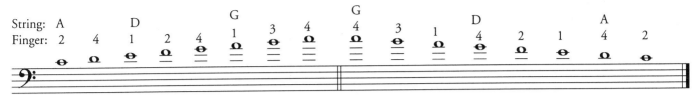

"G" Major Scale

B Blues Scale   F# Blues Scale

Playing in Fourteenth Position

Harmonized "B" Harmonic Minor Scale

Harmonized "C" Major Scale

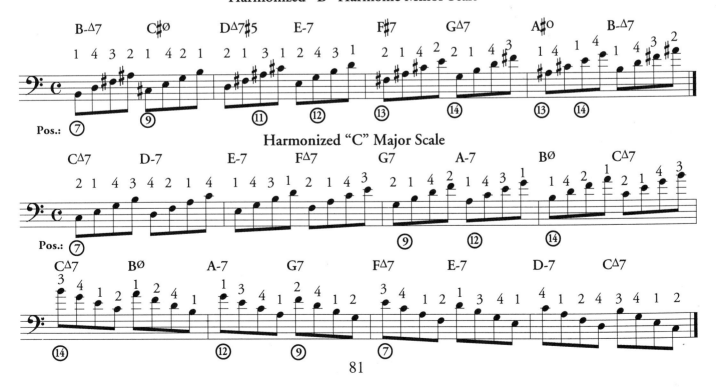

81

Fifteenth Position

Notes, frets, and fingerings for fifteenth position on all four strings

On the "G" string

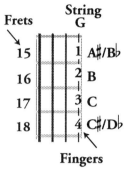

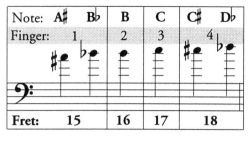

Note:	A♯	B♭	B	C	C♯	D♭
Finger:	1		2	3	4	
Fret:	15		16	17	18	

On the "D" string

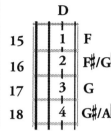

	F	F♯	G♭	G	G♯	A♭
	1	2		3	4	
	15	16		17	18	

On the "A" string

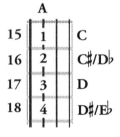

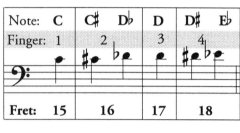

Note:	C	C♯	D♭	D	D♯	E♭
Finger:	1	2		3	4	
Fret:	15	16		17	18	

On the "E" string

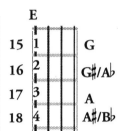

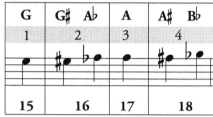

	G	G♯	A♭	A	A♯	B♭
	1	2		3	4	
	15	16		17	18	

---

1   Exercise on G string

2   Exercise on D string

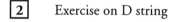

3   Exercise on A string

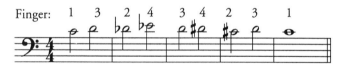

4   Exercise on E string

5   Exercise on all four strings

6

Fifteenth Position

A = 15th Position Basic Studies

B = HARMONIZED, Harmonic Minor and Major Scales (Diatonic 7ths). Positions ⑧ through ⑮, MEMORIZE

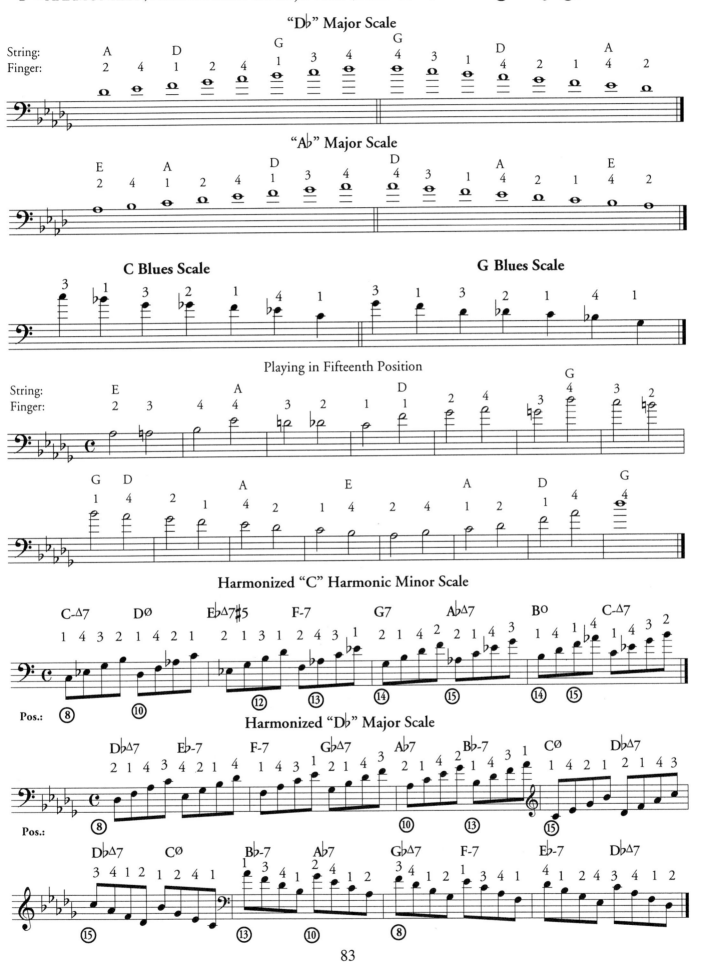

83

Sixteenth Position

Notes, frets, and fingerings for sixteenth position on all four strings

On the "G" string

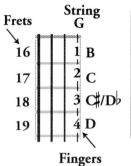

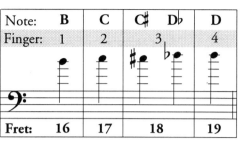

Note:	B	C	C#	Db	D
Finger:	1	2	3		4
Fret:	16	17	18		19

On the "D" string

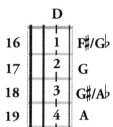

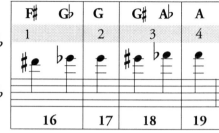

	F#	Gb	G	G#	Ab	A
	1		2	3		4
	16		17	18		19

On the "A" string

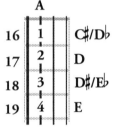

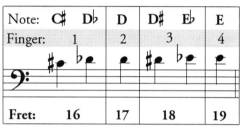

Note:	C#	Db	D	D#	Eb	E
Finger:	1		2	3		4
Fret:	16		17	18		19

On the "E" string

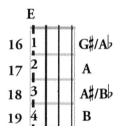

	G#	Ab	A	A#	Bb	B
	1		2	3		4
	16		17	18		19

1 Exercise on G string

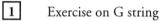

2 Exercise on D string

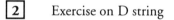

3 Exercise on A string

4 Exercise on E string

5 Exercise on all four strings

6

84

# Sixteenth Position
A = 16th Position Basic Studies
B = HARMONIZED, Harmonic Minor and Major Scales (Diatonic 7ths). Positions ⑨ through ⑯, MEMORIZE

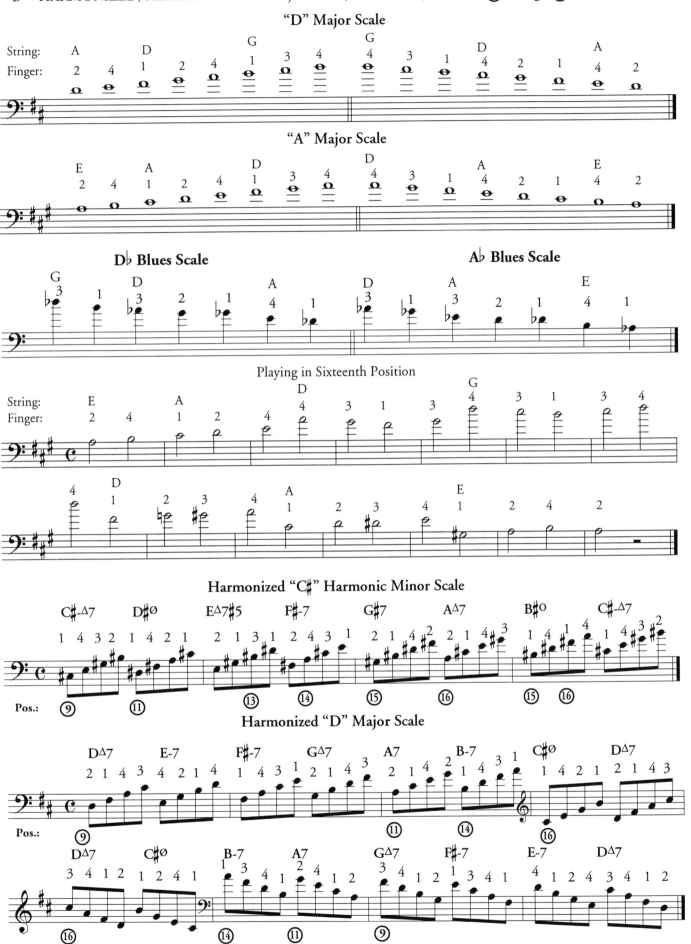

85

Seventeenth Position

Notes, frets, and fingerings for seventeenth position on all four strings

On the "G" string

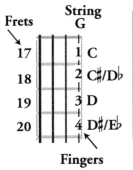
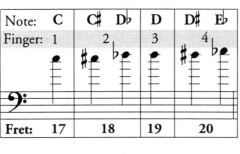

Note:	C	C♯	D♭	D	D♯	E♭
Finger:	1	2		3	4	
Fret:	17	18		19	20	

On the "D" string

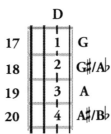
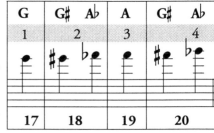

Note:	G	G♯	A♭	A	G♯	A♭
Finger:	1	2		3	4	
Fret:	17	18		19	20	

On the "A" string

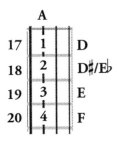
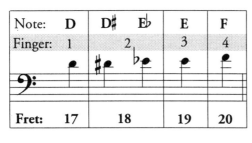

Note:	D	D♯	E♭	E	F
Finger:	1	2		3	4
Fret:	17	18		19	20

On the "E" string

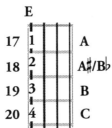
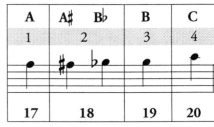

Note:	A	A♯	B♭	B	C
Finger:	1	2		3	4
	17	18		19	20

1 Exercise on G string

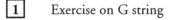

2 Exercise on D string

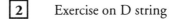

3 Exercise on A string

4 Exercise on E string

5 Exercise on all four strings

6

86

Seventeenth Position

A = 17th Position Basic Studies
B = HARMONIZED, Harmonic Minor and Major Scales (Diatonic 7ths). Positions ⑩ through ⑰, MEMORIZE

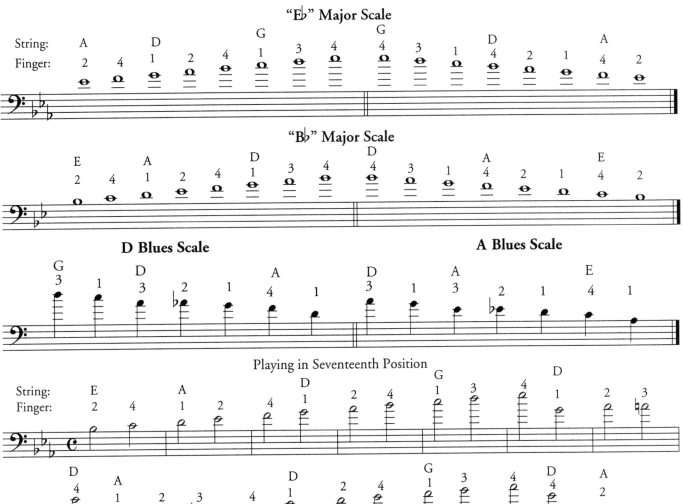

"E♭" Major Scale

"B♭" Major Scale

D Blues Scale

A Blues Scale

Playing in Seventeenth Position

Harmonized "D" Harmonic Minor Scale

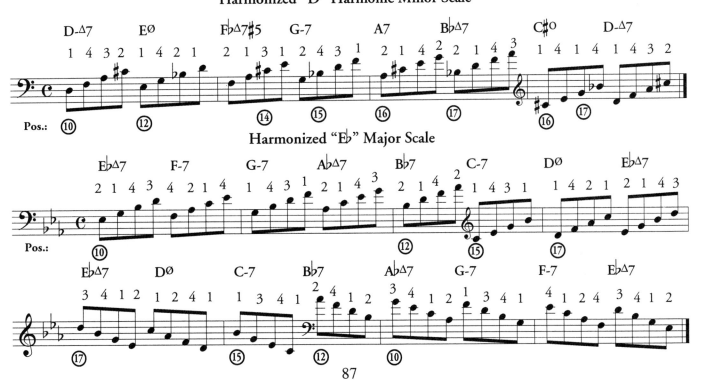

Harmonized "E♭" Major Scale

Various Time Signatures

We will now use unusual meters in studies to prepare the [player to cope with the demands of music written with unusual time signatures.

Study 1: rhythmic variations in 3/4 time.
Study 2: Jazz Waltz using the rhythmic variations in study #1.

Actual Chart Excerpt

To be played in 2nd position except where indicated otherwise

Various Time Signatures

Study 1: rhythmic variations in 6/8 time.
Study 2: Jazz Waltz in 6/8 time.

Actual Chart Excerpt

To be played in 3rd position using C Blues Scale fingering

Various Time Signatures

Study 1: rhythmic variations in 12/8 time which is like playing in slow 4/4 time with triplets.
Study 2: a chart in 12/8 time.

1

Actual Chart Excerpt

To be played in 5th position

2

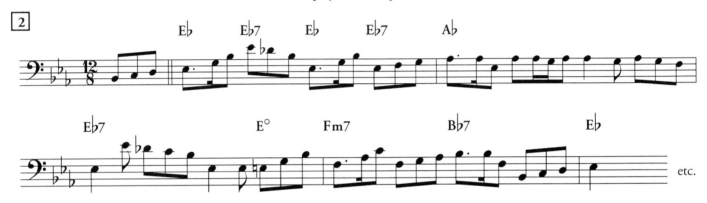

etc.

Study 3: rhythmic variations in 9/8 time which is like playing in slow 3/4 time with triplets.
Study 2: a chart in 9/8 time.

3

Actual Chart Excerpt

To be played in 2nd position

4

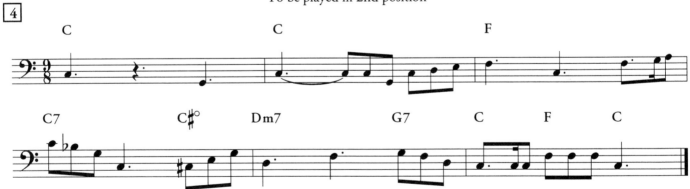

Various Time Signatures

Notice in playing 5/4 time, the accent falls on the 1st and 4th beat

Study 1: rhythmic variations in 5/4 time
Study 2: a chart in 5/4 time.

1

Actual Chart Excerpt

To be played in 5th position

2

91

Various Time Signatures

Notice in 7/4 time the accent falls on the 1st and 5th beat or the 1st, 3rd, and 5th beat

Study 1: rhythmic variations in 7/4 time
Study 2: a chart in 7/4 time.

Actual Chart Excerpt

To be played in 3rd position

Clefs

The bassist should be familiar with these clefs. Oftentimes, because of the ledger lines, the arranger will write in the Treble clef. Very seldom will he write in Tenor clef.

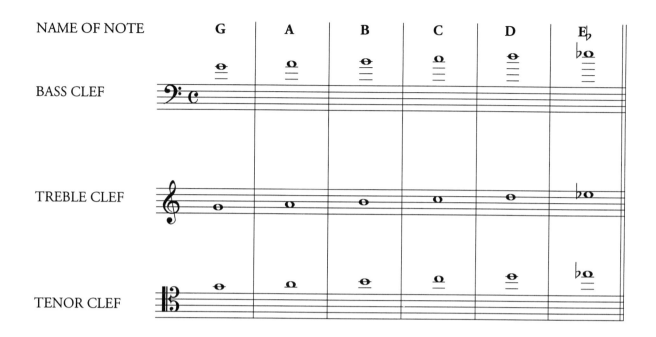

Harmonics

The actual sound of these harmonics are one octave lower.
* Notice location of notes between frets 2 and 3.

Theory for the Bassist

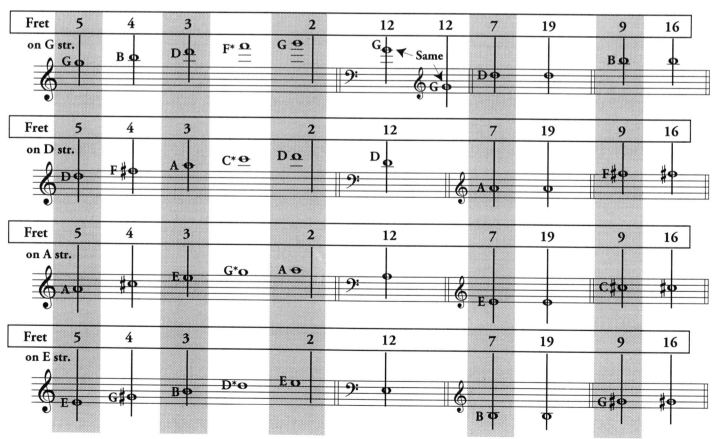

93

Theory for the bassist
How Chords Are Constructed From Scales

1. **Scale:** is a series of musical tones arranged in a specific order ascending or descending.
2. **Chord:** generally three or more notes played together.
3. **Tonic note** or **Keynote:** is the first letter of a major scale.
4. **Octave:** the distance from one tone to the next tone of the same letter name.
5. **Root:** is the chord tone upon which a chord is built.
6. **Scale Degree:** is the numerical order, starting with the tonic note, which is #1, to the octave, which is #8, etc.

MAJOR SCALE CONSTRUCTION
(Using G Major as an Example)

SCALE TONES	G	A	B	C	D	E	F♯	G
SCALE DEGREES	1	2	3	4	5	6	7	8 or 1
INTERVAL DISTANCE BETWEEN SCALE STEPS	W	W	H	W	W	W	H	

W=WHOLE STEP   H=HALF STEP

EXAMPLE: How chords are constructed using a two octave G Major Scale

NOTE		G	A	B	C	D	E	F♯	G	A	B	C	D	E	F♯	G
Scale Degree		1	2	3	4	5	6	7	8	9	10	11	12	13	14	15
Chord Symbol	G	1		3		5										
	Gm	1		♭3		5										
	G+	1		3		♯5										
	G°7	1		♭3		♭5	6									
	G7	1		3		5		♭7								
	Gm7	1		♭3		5		♭7								
	GMaj.7	1		3		5		7								
	G∅	1		♭3		♭5		♭7								
	G9	1		3		5		♭7		9						
	G11	1		3		5		♭7		9		11				
	G13	1		3		5		♭7		9		11		13		

Chord Name	Symbol	Chord Construction	Formula
Major		Root, 3rd, and 5th	R 3 5
Minor	m	Root, lower 3rd 1/2 tone, and 5th	R ♭3 5
Augmented	+	Root, 3rd, and raise 5th 1/2 tone	R 3 ♯5
Diminished7	°7	Root, lower 3rd 1/2 tone, lower 5th 1/2 tone, and 6th	R ♭3 ♭5 6
7th	7	Root, 3rd, 5th, and lower 7th 1/2 tone	R 3 5 ♭7
Minor 7	m7	Root, lower 3rd 1/2 tone, 5th, and lower 7th 1/2 tone	R ♭3 5 ♭7
Major 7	Maj7 or 7	Root, 3rd, 5th, and 7th	R ♭3 ♭5 7
Half Diminished	∅	Root, lower 3rd 1/2 tone, lower 5th 1/2 tone, and lower 7th 1/2 tone	R ♭3 ♭5 ♭7

The Twelve Major Scales

MEMORIZE the Twelve Major Scales by the letter name and the scale degree. Chords are constructed by extracting scale degrees from the major scale.

EXAMPLE: the notes in a G major chord are G B D, hence the formula is 1 (which is root) 3 5. To transpose to a major chord in another key, use the formula 1 3 5. Thus, a C major chord is C E G, and an F major chord is F A C etc. The best method of study is to take one scale a day, and memorize that scale, and write out both the number and letter name.

EXAMPLE: G 7
        1 3 5 $\flat$7
        G B D F

NOTE: The 9th has the same letter name as 2
              The 11th has the same letter name as 4
              The 13th has the same letter name as 6

SCALE DEGREE	1	2	3	4	5	6	7	8 or 1
	C	D	E	F	G	A	B	C
1 FLAT	F	G	A	B$\flat$	C	D	E	F
2 FLATS	B$\flat$	C	D	E$\flat$	F	G	A	B$\flat$
3 FLATS	E$\flat$	F	G	A$\flat$	B$\flat$	C	D	E$\flat$
4 FLATS	A$\flat$	B$\flat$	C	D$\flat$	E$\flat$	F	G	A$\flat$
5 FLATS	D$\flat$	E$\flat$	F	G$\flat$	A$\flat$	B$\flat$	C	D$\flat$
6 FLATS	G$\flat$	A$\flat$	B$\flat$	C$\flat$	D$\flat$	E$\flat$	F	G$\flat$
5 SHARPS	B	C$\sharp$	D$\sharp$	E	F$\sharp$	G$\sharp$	A$\sharp$	B
4 SHARPS	E	F$\sharp$	G$\sharp$	A	B	C$\sharp$	D$\sharp$	E
3 SHARPS	A	B	C$\sharp$	D	E	F$\sharp$	G$\sharp$	A
2 SHARPS	D	E	F$\sharp$	G	A	B	C$\sharp$	D
1 SHARP	G	A	B	C	D	E	F$\sharp$	G

A CHART USING G TYPE CHORDS
How To Construct Chords By Extracting Scale Degrees

MEMORIZE THIS CHART

Chord Symbol	G	Gm	G°7	G+	G7	Gm7
Scale Degree	1 3 5	1 $\flat$3 5	1 $\flat$3 $\flat$5 6	1 $\flat$3 $\sharp$5	1 3 5 $\flat$7	1 $\flat$3 5 $\flat$7

Chord Symbol	G7+5	G7$\flat$5	GMaj7	Gm+7	Gm7$\flat$5 or ∅
Scale Degree	1 3 $\sharp$5 $\flat$7	1 3 $\flat$5 $\flat$7	1 3 5 7	1 $\flat$3 5 7	1 $\flat$3 $\flat$5 $\flat$7

Chord Symbol	G7sus4	G6	Gm6	G9	Gm9
Scale Degree	1 4 5 $\flat$7	1 3 5 6	1 $\flat$3 5 6	1 3 5 $\flat$7 9	1 $\flat$3 5 $\flat$7 9

Chord Symbol	GMaj9	G9+5	G9$\flat$5	G7$\flat$9
Scale Degree	1 3 5 7 9	1 3 $\sharp$5 $\flat$7 9	1 3 $\flat$5 $\flat$7 9	1 3 5 $\flat$7 $\flat$9

Chord Symbol	G7+9	G$\frac{9}{6}$	G11	G11+
Scale Degree	1 3 5 $\flat$7 $\sharp$9	1 3 5 6 9	1 3 5 $\flat$7 9 11	1 3 5 $\flat$7 9 $\sharp$11

Chord Symbol	G13	G13$\flat$9
Scale Degree	1 3 5 $\flat$7 9 11 13	1 3 5 $\flat$7 $\flat$9 11 13

95

Theory for the Bassist

I want to stress here the necessity of memorizing the notes and scale degrees of the twelve scales. By being able to relate chord symbols to numbers, the musician is able to talk about chord progressions in the abstract (chord relationships that are good for any key).

How to Relate Chord Symbols and Numbers

Music written in the key of G: all G chords are numbered I. All A chords are numbered II, and all B chords are numbered III etc... The chord number is the same as the scale note number.

EXAMPLE:

Harmonized G Scales
Triads

1 3 5   1 ♭3 5

I	II	III	IV	V	VI	VII°
G	Am	Bm	C	D	Em	F♯m♭5

Diatonic 7ths

1 3 5 7   1 ♭3 5 ♭7

IMa7	IIm7	IIIm7	IVMa7	V7	VIm7	VII°
GMa7	Am7	Bm7	CMa7	D7	Em7	F♯m7♭5

Secondary Dominants

1 3 5 ♭7

I6	II7	III7	IV7	V7	VI7	VII°
G6	A7	B7	C7	D7	E7	F♯m7♭5

Harmonized Minor Scales in Diatonic 7ths
Natural

I	II	III	IV	V	VI	VII
G-7	Aø	B♭Δ7	C-7	D-7	E♭Δ7	F7

Harmonic

I	II	III	IV	V	VI	VII
G-Δ7	Aø	B♭Δ7♯5	C-7	D7	E♭Δ7	F♯°7

Ascending Melodic Minor

I	II	III	IV	V	VI	VII
G-Δ7	A-7	B♭Δ7♯5	C7	D7	Eø	F♯ø

Actual Chord Progressions showing how the number and letter names relate

I	IMa7	I7	IV	IVm	V7	I
G	GMa7	G7	C	Cm	D7	G

Im	Im+7	Im7	Im6	IVm	V7	Im
Gm	Gm+7	Gm7	Gm6	Cm	D7	Gm

Theory for the Bassist

Now that you have memorized the twelve major scales and the chart on How To Construct Chords, the next step is playing the arpeggios. The following studies are chord diagrams with the fingering patterns and note names. I strongly urge you to Memorize the Sound. Do not just learn the fingering pattern for a chord, be able to sing it. If studied this way the fingering and the sound will be as one. The ultimate goal is being able to look at a chord symbol and know the sound, before you play it, and how it is played. This takes practice.

The scales and arpeggios are likened to the foundation of a building. That is, without a good foundation the building will not stand. So the bassist needs a good foundation in order to perform in every given musical situation.
Diagrams for the G and C fingerings are used here to speed the learning process, of the arpeggios. Practice playing chromatically up the fingerboard, be aware of the notes you are playing.

As you proceed in these studies, you will learn to play arpeggios and scales several ways, by rearranging the notes. You will then have the choice of bass lines you prefer, also the ability to add non chordal notes to make interesting bass lines.

Using the G Arpeggio as an Example:

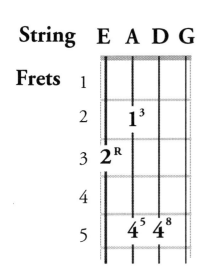

Using the G Arpeggio as an Example: Order in which the diagram should be practiced,

Ascending	Descending
1. 2nd finger on E string	5. 4th finger on D string
2. 1st finger on A string	6. 4th finger on A string
3. 4th finger on A string	7. 1st finger on A string
4. 4th finger on D string	8. 2nd finger on E string

Practice playing the G and C Arpeggios in a slow even tempo that is comfortable for you. As you become familiar with the fingerings, increase the tempo.

Theory for the Bassist
Diagrams For G Arpeggio
All fingering patterns are movable
TRANSPOSITION CHART

Fret	3	4	5	6	7	8	9	10	11	12
Chord	G	A♭	A	B♭	B	C	D♭	D	E♭	E

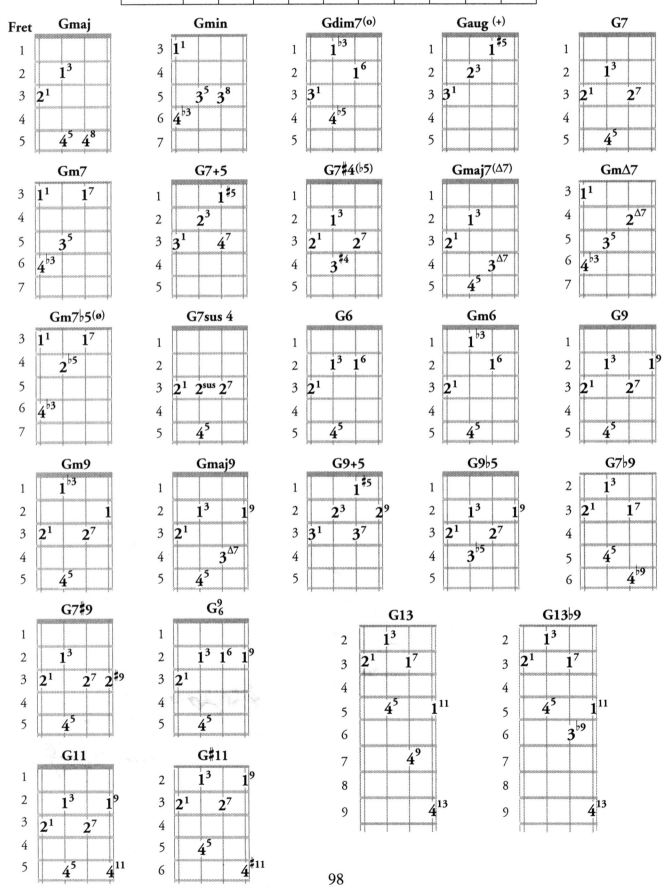

Theory for the Bassist
Diagrams For C Arpeggio
All fingering patterns are movable
TRANSPOSITION CHART

Fret	3	4	5	6	7	8	9	10	11	12
Chord	C	D♭	D	E♭	E	F	G♭	G	A♭	A

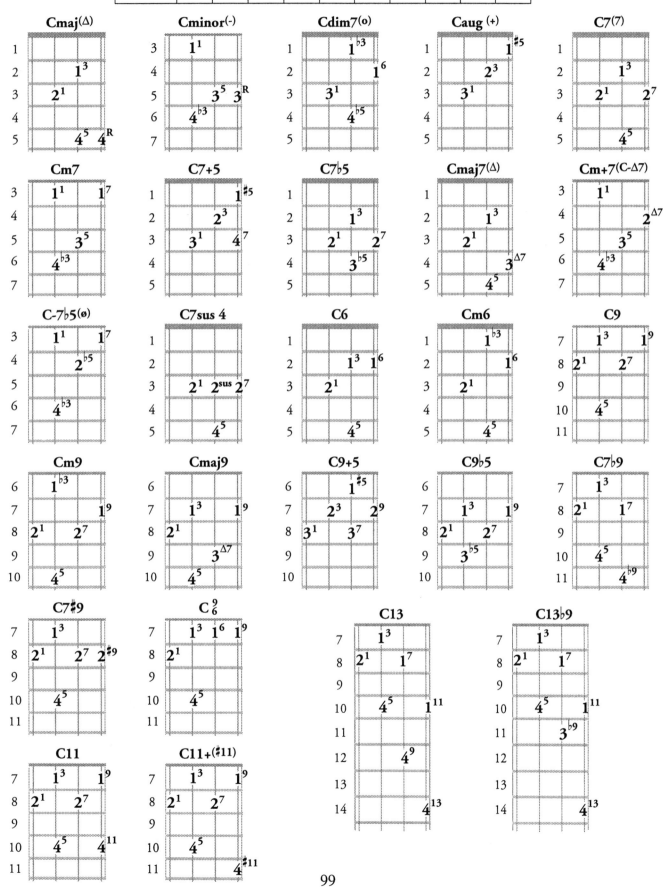

99

Modes of the Major, Harmonic Minor, and Ascending (Jazz) Melodic Minor Scales

Understanding the function of modes and where they originate (parent key) is most helpful to anyone who intends to improvise. Many of the most commonly used modes and the chord they generate are in the Scale and Arpeggio (Chords) section of the position studies (position two through eight). Learn the modal scales and chords as well as they are powerful arsenal for ideas, rhythm section and soloing.

Mode	C Major Scale	Related Chords														
1	Ionian	C, C∆7, C6, C9, C6/9, Csus	C	D	E	F	G	A	B	C						
2	Dorian	D-, D-7, D-9, D-11, D-6		D	E	F	G	A	B	C	D					
3	Phrygian	E-, E-7, E-7♭9			E	F	G	A	B	C	D	E				
4	Lydian	F∆7, F∆7♯11, F∆9, F6/9				F	G	A	B	C	D	E	F			
5	Mixolydian	G7, G9, G11, G13					G	A	B	C	D	E	F	G		
6	Aeolian	A-, A-7, A-9, A-11						A	B	C	D	E	F	G	A	
7	Locrian	B-7♭5 (ø half diminished)							B	C	D	E	F	G	A	B

Mode	C Jazz Melodic Minor	Related Chords														
1	Jazz Mel. Minor	C-, C-∆7 (C-+7)	C	D	E♭	F	G	A	B	C						
2	Dorian ♭2	D-, D7♭9, D7♯9		D	E♭	F	G	A	B	C	D					
3	Lydian Augmented	E♭∆7♯5			E♭	F	G	A	B	C	D	E♭				
4	Lydian ♭7	F, F9, F13, F7♯11, F7♭5, F13♯11				F	G	A	B	C	D	E♭	F			
5	Mixolydian ♭6	G7, G7♯5, G7♭13, G9♯5					G	A	B	C	D	E♭	F	G		
6	Locrian #2	Aø (minor7♭5)						A	B	C	D	E♭	F	G	A	
7	Super Locrian (diminished whole tone)	B7♯9, B7♭9, B7♭9♭5, B7♯9♯5, B7♭9♯5, B7♯9♭5, B7 alt.							B	C	D	E♭	F	G	A	B

The most commonly used modes other than the parent scales are: Lydian Augmented, Lydian ♭7, Locrian #2, and Super Locrian (all are included in the Scale and Arpeggio (Chords) section of the position studies (position two through eight).

Modes of the Harmonic Minor Scale

There are no universal names for the modes of the harmonic minor scales such as Dorian, Lydian, etc. They are identified by their numerical position in the scale, HM4, HM5 (short for harmonic scale minor 4th mode or harmonic min. 5th mode).

Mode	C Harmonic Minor	Related Chords														
	C Harmonic Minor	C-, C-∆7, C-add9	C	D	E♭	F	G	A♭	B	C						
HM2	C HM2	Dø (m7♭5)		D	E♭	F	G	A♭	B	C	D					
HM3	C HM3	E♭∆7♯5, E♭+			E♭	F	G	A♭	B	C	D	E♭				
HM4	C HM4	F-, F-6, F-6/9, F-7				F	G	A♭	B	C	D	E♭	F			
HM5	C HM5	G7♭9, G7♯5, G7♭9♭5, G7sus					G	A♭	B	C	D	E♭	F	G		
HM6	C HM6	A♭∆7, A♭∆7♯11						A♭	B	C	D	E♭	F	G	A♭	
HM7	C HM7	B° (diminished)							B	C	D	E♭	F	G	A♭	B

The most commonly used modes of the harmonic minor scales are HM2, HM4 and HM5.

Ear Development
Intervals

Be able to recognize intervals both visually and aurally when seen or heard. Memorize their sound and be able to PLAY and SING them ascending and descending from each of the twelve chromatic pitches.

1. Practice playing and singing all intervals   **2. Study: for pre-hearing, do with all intervals up and down**

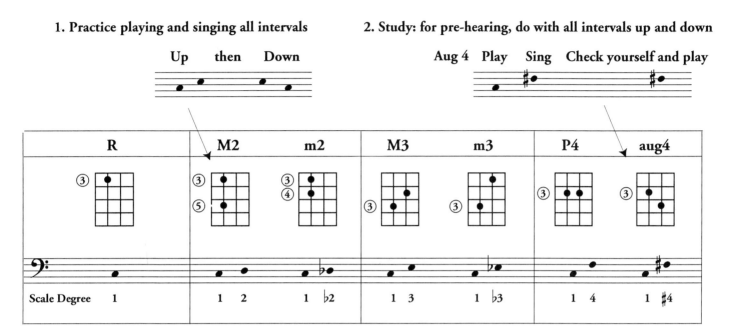

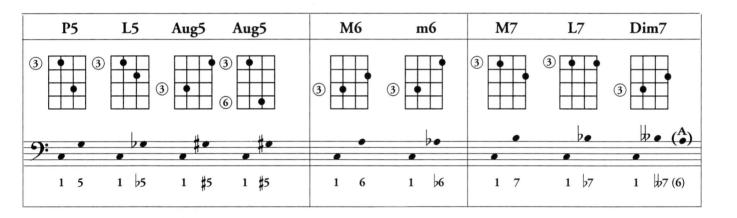

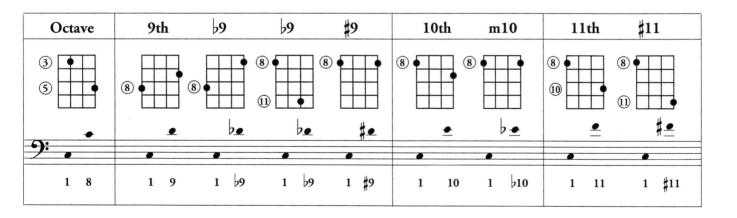

101

I IV V Chord Progression

The I IV V progression is one of the most basic and quite possibly the most used chord progression, from traditional blues, to jazz, to western music.
It makes sense to start playing chord progressions from chord symbols or chord numerals.
I recommend that you memorize the chart below.

I IV V CHART IN ALL KEYS		
I	**IV**	**V**
C	F	G7
D♭	G♭	A♭7
D	G	A7
E♭	A♭	B♭7
E	A	B7
F	B♭	C7
G♭	C♭	D♭7
G	C	D7
A♭	D♭	E♭7
A	D	E7
B♭	E♭	F7
B	E	F♯7

I IV V Chord Progression

Practice playing up chromatically as far as the fingerboard will allow, always being aware of what notes are being played. Then play in all 12 keys.

Using Roots and Fifths

Use with: major-minor-and dominant chords that don't have an altered fifth (♯ or ♭).

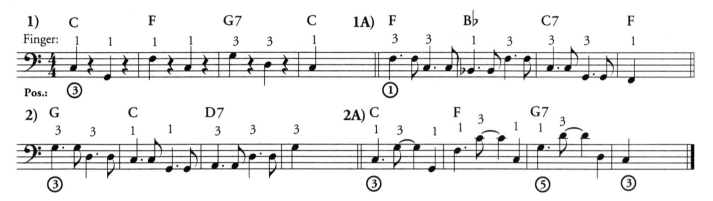

Using the Root, Third, and Fifths

Use with: major and dominant chords that don't have an altered fifth (♯ or ♭).

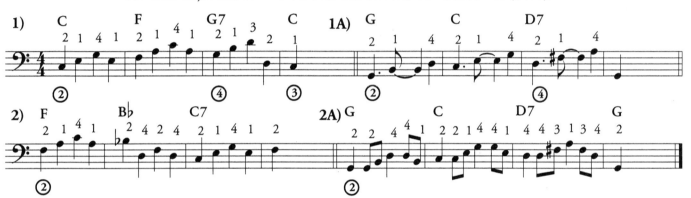

One position ③ traditional I IV V blues progression. MEMORIZE fingering and transpose to other keys

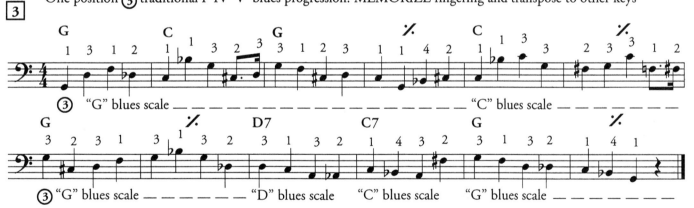

Two chord progression I IV, using patterns taken from the "G" and "C" Mixolydian scale

I IV V Chord Progression

A Contrast of Style Using I IV I

Traditional blues progression in "E" Maj. using syncopated rhythms E7 A7 B7

I IV V

Traditional blues progression in "F" Maj. using Walking Bass and some rhythmic variations

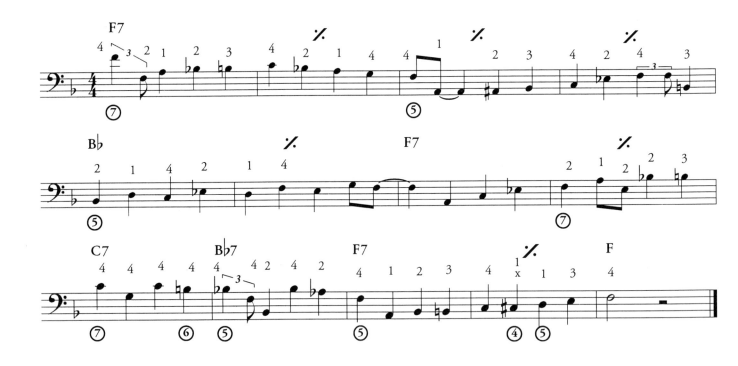

Pop-Rock, Blues I IV V Progression

On these type tunes establish a feel with the drummer, also know what the vocal is doing and play off it also by filling in the open spots yet maintaining the groove.

Numbers 1 and 2 are played at the same tempo but the feel is totally different. Number 1 is a driving pattern. #2 is a little more laid back.

For the <u>Slow Blues</u> 12/8 (4/4) see the triplet studies in first position and the 12/8 in the various time signature section.

Dominant Chord Scales use with 2 Measure Dominant 7th Progressions

These versatile scales work well with accompaniment and soloing due to the lines and chords they generate. MASTER THEM in all 12 keys. The chord progressions use only notes extracted from the given scales.

"G" Mixolydian Scale

"C" Diminished Whole Tone Scale (Super Locrian)

"F" Lydian Dominant Scale

"Bb" Diminished Scale 1/2 Step Whole Step

"Eb" Whole Tone Scale

106

Two Bar Dominant Seventh Patterns

Be aware of scales degrees. Then play in all 12 keys

Syncopated Patterns (Mixolydian Scale Patterns)

Walking bass pattern using the whole tone scale, used normally with a dominant 7th that has a raised or lowered 5th or both. Also an augmented triad with a dominant function.

*Ab Augmented triad

A note reading tip: on beats ♩♪♩♩ slightly anticipate the 4th beat with the preceeding sixteen note Think of it as belonging to the 4th beat.

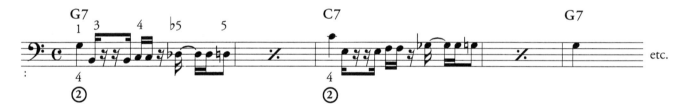

II V Latin Patterns

107

II V I Chord Progression
or
II V Chord Progression

This is another popular and important chord progression.

A II V progression is a minor 7th going to a dominant 7th a fourth above or a fifth below, which would bear the same chord name.

Some tunes will change keys several times. If you learn to read chords in groups or clusters, you will be able to pick out the II V, the I VI II V, or whatever groups of progressions are used.

Then, you will be able to create from a group of chords, rather than one at the time; hence, developing good reading habits and quick, spontaneous bass lines.

The Major II V I chords are derived from the Major Scale.

The Minor IIØ V I chords are derived from the Harmonic Minor Scale.

MEMORIZE

Excerpts of actual chord progression

(II V I in G Maj)				(II V I in F Maj)			
II	**V**	**I**	**I**	**II**	**V**	**I**	**I**
A-7	D7	G	٪	G-7	C7	F	٪

Excerpts of actual chord progression

(IIØ V I in A min)			(IIØ V I in D min)		
II	**V**	**I**	**II**	**V**	**II**	**V**	**I**
BØ	E7♭9	A-	BØ	E7	EØ	A7♭9	D-

Major

II V I CHART IN ALL KEYS		
IIm7	**V7**	**I**
Dm7	G7	C
E♭m7	A♭7	D♭
Em7	A7	D
Fm7	B♭7	E♭
F♯m7	B7	E
Gm7	C7	F
A♭m7	D♭7	G♭
Am7	D7	G
B♭m7	E♭7	A♭
Bm7	E7	A
Cm7	F7	B♭
C♯m7	F♯7	B

Minor

IIØ V I CHART IN ALL KEYS		
Half Diminished **IIm7♭5 or ø**	(9 is flat: ♭9) **V**	**I**
DØ	G7(♭9)	C-(m)
E♭Ø	A♭7(♭9)	D♭-
EØ	A7(♭9)	D-
FØ	B♭7(♭9)	E♭-
F♯Ø	B7(♭9)	E-
GØ	C7(♭9)	F-
A♭Ø	D♭7(♭9)	G♭-
AØ	D7(♭9)	G-
B♭Ø	E♭7(♭9)	A♭-
BØ	E7(♭9)	A-
CØ	F7(♭9)	B♭-
C♯Ø	F♯7(♭9)	B-

II V I and IIØ V I Progressions

The scale degrees (digital patterns) are listed over every note. Pick a pattern or patterns that are comfortable and play them in all 12 keys; this is also great ear training.

IIØ V I in Minor Keys

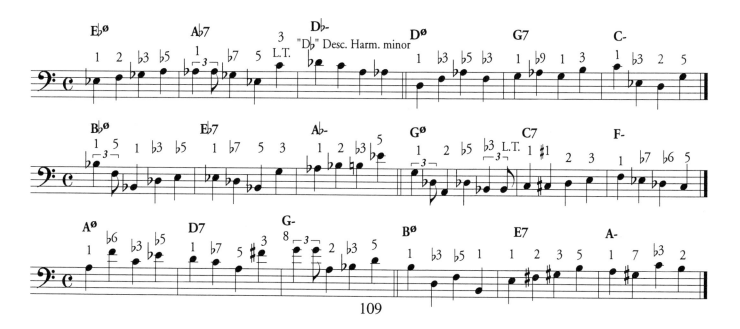

IIm7 V7 and II7 V7 Chord Progressions
Multi-Chordal Bass Lines

These versatile bass lines for two chord per measure, 1, 2, 3 and 4 will work with any combination of II V progressions, as the only scale degrees being used are the 1, 3, ♭7, and leading tones, therefore not clashing with any chordal alteration. Explanation of #5 is above progression study.

PRACTICE these patterns on various areas of the fingerboard, 8va, etc.; also use various rhythmic variations:

MEMORIZE progressions 1 through 4

Leading Tones From 1/2 Step Above

Leading Tones From 1/2 Step Below

When playing accompaniment it is usually best to leave the upper alterations of a dominant chord (♯9, ♭9, etc.) To the soloist, keyboard or other chordal instrument. However, DO play the altered 5ths (♯5, ♭5) as this will identify the desired dominant 7th.

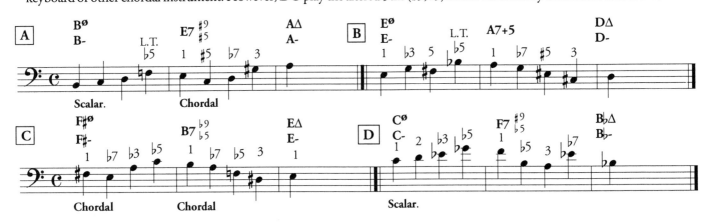

110

BeBop Era Blues Progressions

This blues is very characteristic of many of the BeBop era tunes: short chord durations, digital patterns (1, ♭3, 13), quickly changing keys, turnarounds, II V progressions, and chromatic and cycle progressions.

I (VI AND VI7) II V Chord Progressions
Two Chords Per Measure

The Ⓐ, Ⓑ, Ⓒ, etc. lines can be played individually (double bars) or straight through. Most of the I VI II V progressions are usually 4 measures. For 4 bar practice one could play the first 4 bars or combine different combinations: Ⓐ and Ⓔ, Ⓓ and Ⓕ, etc. REMEMBER, be aware of those scale DEGREES. Learn as many lines as possible in all 12 keys.

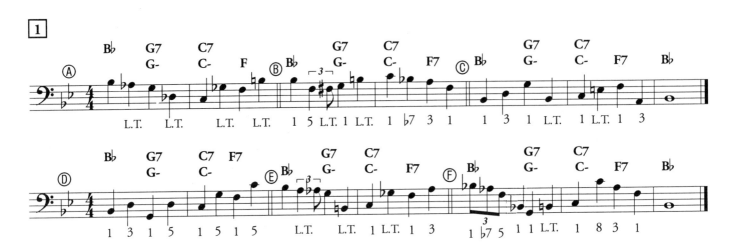

Notice at letter Ⓒ measures 3 and 4 start on the 3rd and ♭3rd, creating a very smooth bass line.

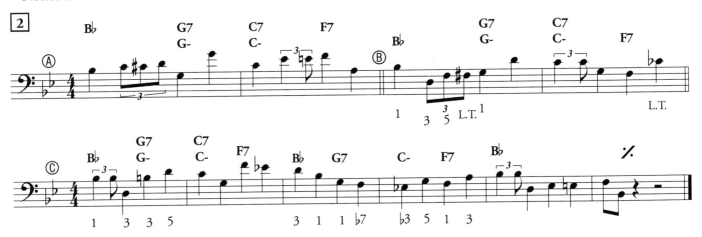

Two 4-measure lines. The 3rd in measure 5 is anticipated in measure 4 on the fourth beat,

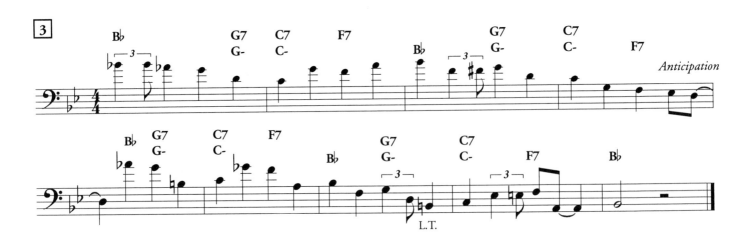

I (VI AND VI7) II V Chord Progressions
One Chord Per Measure

Observe: scale degrees, leading tones (L.T.) and written words. Using this as a base, transpose these lines and patterns to other keys. Then, try creating your own lines over the I VI II V progression.

Walkin Bass, one chord per measure

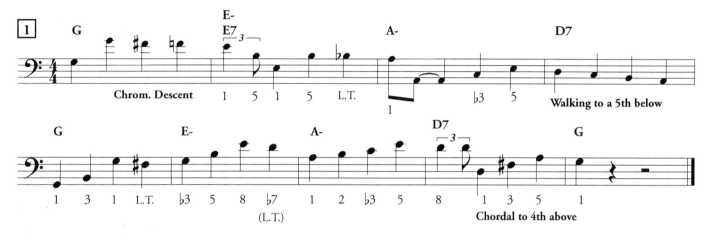

Smooth Syncopated rhythm patterns. 2A uses a I VI IV V progression

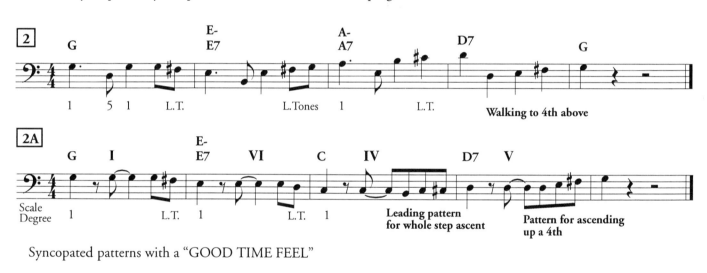

Syncopated patterns with a "GOOD TIME FEEL"

113

I VI7 II7 V7 Chord Progression
Various Styles

#3, deadened string technique: mute the x's with the left hand (put finger over given note marked "x" but do not depress the note.

#4 is a shuffle written ♫ but played ♪♪ .

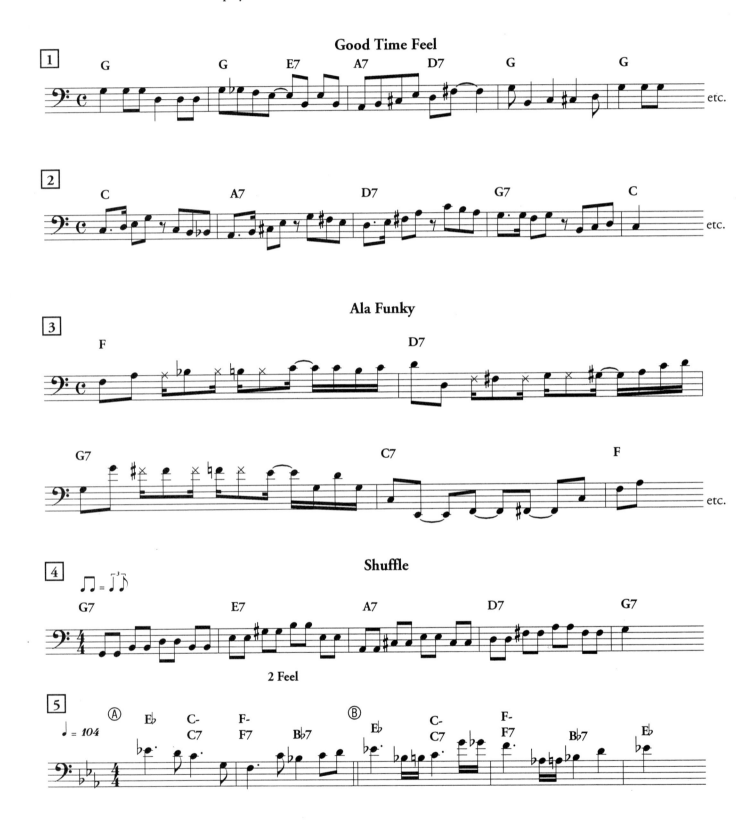

114

I ♯Iº IIm7 V7 Chord Progression
A Standard Tune

Using the I ♯Iº II ♯IIº, I I7 IV IVm, I VI II V plus a III7 VI7 II V turnaround all in the first 8 measures.

The tune is an AABA form. The first 8 bars repeat AA; the B section, referred to as the Bridge; then the last 8 bars, the same as A.

On the "2 feel" the 8th note preceding a quarter note gives the feel a "lift." Notice in measures 5 and 8 half notes and quarter notes are used. This gives the rhythm a "breather" from the pushing 8th note. Mix them up, as this makes both of them effective and avoids monotony of sound.

Important scale degrees and Leading Tones (L.T.) are shown.

I ♯I° IIm7 V7 Chord Progression

Walking lines to a jazz standard. Analyze scale degrees, leading tones, etc. as this will aid greatly in transposing this progression and lines to ALL 12 keys

Latin, Bossa Nova

I ♯Iº IIm7 V7 Chord Progression

More lines showing the effectiveness of the scale degrees and chord tones (the right notes). Learn #7 in ALL 12 keys, then try transposing some of the others. Try some of your own lines over the chord changes.

Latin Rhythms

117

I Ima7 IV IVm V7 Chord Progression

In this type progression try to outline the chromatic melodic motion of the chordal pattern (1 7 b7 3 b3 1) by uniting them with the root motion of the progression.

G	F#	F	E	Eb	D
I	IΔ7	I7	IV	IV	V
G	GΔ7	G7	C	C-	D7

Be able to recognize and play this chordal pattern in ALL 12 keys

118

I Imaj7 I6 I Chord Progression

Be aware of scale degrees, then play in all 12 keys.
Playing off of the chordal melodic motion: I, Δ7, 6, and I

I	Δ7	6	1/5
D	C#	B	A

Three Latin Patterns: Ⓐ Ⓑ Ⓒ and one syncopated pattern

Basic Rhythm Patterns bringing out the descending line

3/4 Patterns and 4/4 Walking Bass Lines bringing out the prominent (I- Δ7- 6) notes of the progression.

119

Im Im+7 Im7 Im6 Chord Progression

This chord progression can also be used as a substitute progression when the same minor chord is used for 2, 3, or 4, measures.

In this type of chord progression, try to outline the chromatic melodic motion of the chordal pattern (I, Δ7, ♭7, 6) by uniting them with the root motion of the chordal sequence.

Be able to recognize and play these chordal patterns in ALL 12 keys

Walking Bass Lines. Add rhythmic variation: etc.

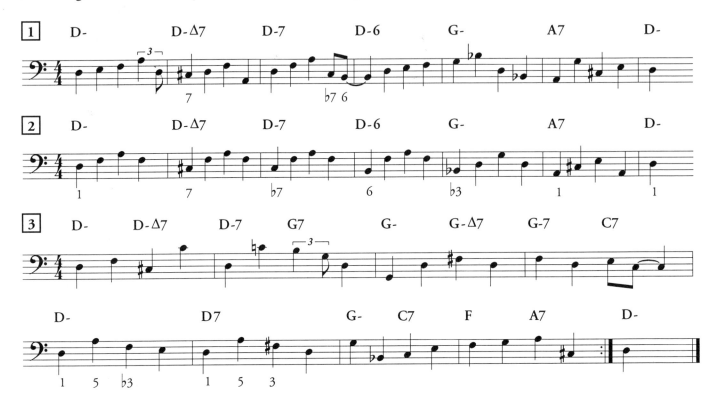

On #4 notice the power of the root and 5th. The notes in parenthesis (♯●) are played by the higher instruments, keyboards etc. Numbers 4, 5, and 6 are applicable to any tempo and are very effective on ballads (♩= *60* to *80*).

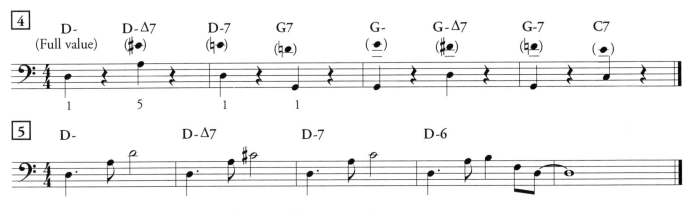

Playing off the descending line using chromatic fill. Use sparingly.

Im Im+7 Im7 Im6 Chord Progression

This chord progression can also be used as a substitute progression when the same minor chord is used for 2, 3, or 4 measures.

Latin Rhythm

Number 5 is a TUMBOA, a repeated figure that establishes the groove. This is also how most Montunos (a repeated pattern of one or two chords) are played. Here we are using a Tumboa figure over a chord progression.

Pianistic type patterns. Nice for intros' before rhythm patterns (above) or unison with lead instruments.
Sections Ⓐ and Ⓑ are to be played in 4th position, making it a movable bar line for other keys.
This "tune" unites the I-ImΔ7-Im7-Im6 progression with the I-IΔ7-I6.

I II ♯II° IIIm7 Chord Progression

This chord progression can also be used as a substitute progression when a major chord is played for two consecutive measures.

Be aware of scale degrees, then play in all 12 keys.

Using Roots (I) and 5ths

Using 3rds and Triads. Add rhythmic variations [♩ ♪♪ ♩ ♩ ♩] etc. to walking lines but don't overuse them.

3/4 Time

Two Syncopated Patterns

122

Actual Chart Using Notes and Chord Symbols

This chart gives you the opportunity to apply what you've previously learned about reading chords in groups or clusters as discussed in the II V and I II ♯II° IIIm progressions. The "A" Section is played with a "2" feel, using whole step — half step — leading tones from above and below in the first three measures.

* Play suggested scale degrees first. Then make up your own.

123

I I7 IV IVm V7 Chord Progression
Walking and 2 Feel Bass Lines
Chordal Melodic Motion: 1, ♭7, 3, ♭3

Practice playing up chromatically as far as the fingerboard will allow.

A popular line for this progression.

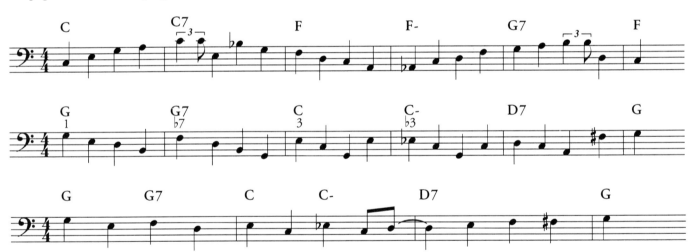

Playing this progression in the higher register. Transpose some of the above lines up the neck.

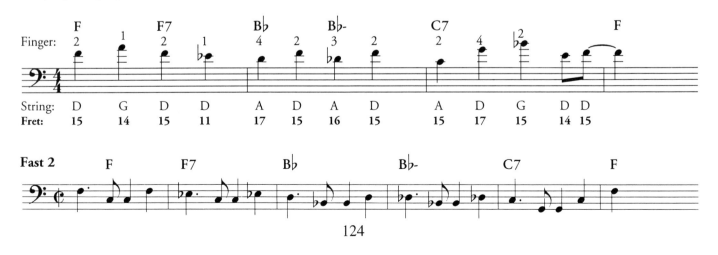

I I7 IV IVm V7 Chord Progression

Study 1: the chord change is on every beat, so play chordal melodic motion.
Study 2: a rock pattern with arranger's indicated rhytm pattern.

Practice playing up chromatically as far as the fingerboard will allow.

I I7 IV IVm V7 Chord Progression

Study 1: soft rock pattern emphasizing the chordal melodic motion.
Study 2: commercial rock pattern playing off the prevailing line.

Practice playing up chromatically as far as the fingerboard will allow.

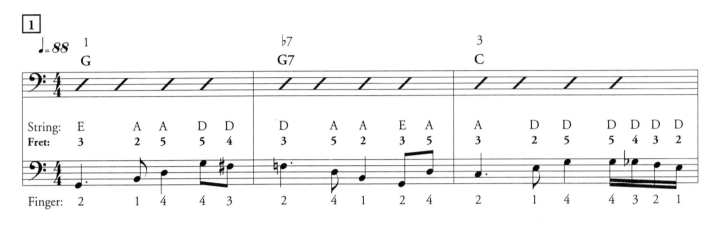

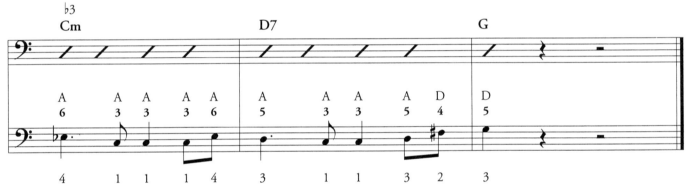

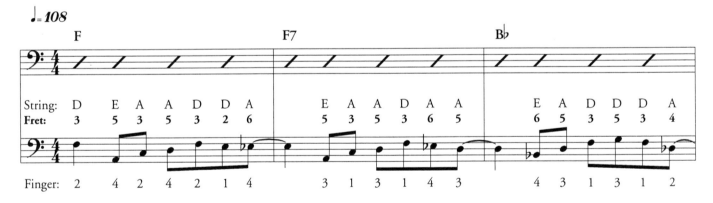

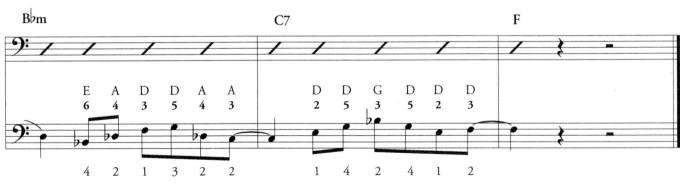

126

I III7 VI7 II7 V7 Chord Progression
A Standard Tune

This tune will demonstrate playing in the traditional Dixieland "2" beat style. The bridge (Ⓑ) is usually played in walking "4". Then, the final Ⓐ section in "2". On the lead solos the bass plays a walking "4" with rhythmic variations.

Walking lines for the Ⓐ sections of the above tunes

I III7 VI7 II7 V7 I Chord Progression

Having seen this progression in a "2" beat Dixieland style, we will now put it in a more contemporary setting.

I II III II Chord Progression

Using both chordal and scalar lines in Latin, walking and the syncopated rhythms that are so necessary to master in contemporary playing.

This progression is sometimes used as a substitute when the "I" chord lasts for two measures. Use the two chord per measure lines.

The following lines should be transposed to ALL 12 keys.

A Jazz Standard Modal Tune

A modal tune extends for long durations over one chord/scale. Try to play in two-bar phrases, root on the downbeat of every other bar.

A good way to proclaim the root sound. It is best however to mix these two-bar phrases with an occasional four-bar phrase (first four bars of Eb- and the last six bars of the tune.) Do not overuse the four-bar phrase.

While the Dorian mode is the main scale, notice how effective it is to flat the 6th and play half step leading tones, very sparingly. Do not overuse, keep it modal. It is not II V Be Bop.

Chord Progression to a Jazz Standard

Rhythm Section Bass

Things to notice: Ⓐ bars 1 and 2 brings out the 6th; bars 3,4,11 and 12 using the whole tone scale bring out the ♯11 and ♯5; and bars 5 and 6 using a very useful II and V line.

In the Ⓑ section (bridge) the 1st and 3rd bars are the same line one octave apart, bars 5 and 6 quote a melody (Sweet Georgia Brown), bars 7 and 8 the Dorian scale in 3rds.

The last Ⓐ section, bars 1 and 2 use a descending Be Bop major scale (8 7 6 ♭6 5 4 3 2 1). Bars 3 and 4, a Lydian dominant scale brings out the ♯11.

Chord Progression to a Standard Bossa Nova

Using four different approaches accompanying this type tune. The first and second Ⓐ sections vary the basic bossa beat (♩. ♪ ♩. ♪) using fills, yet maintaining the feel and leading to the next chord musically. The Ⓑ section starts with a fill then goes straight ahead basic. In the final Ⓐ section the root, third and fifth give a big full sound when played in the lower register.

132

Jazz -Rock and Funk Playing

Deadened String Technique

In jazz/rock one of the techniques a bassist should master is learning to deaden the string with the left hand while still playing the right hand. In order to deaden a note or string, put the left hand finger directly on the note to be played without actually depressing the string. This deadened string technique is very useful when reading charts with difficult syncopation. When using this technique, merely use the left hand to deaden the string on the rests while playing them through with the right hand.

Mastering this technique enables the bassist to more accurately play "off beat" and accented notes, without losing the "feel", and gives the pattern a special effect sound, plus a great lift.

Rhythm Patterns
Jazz-Rock

Employing Deadened String Technique (muffled)

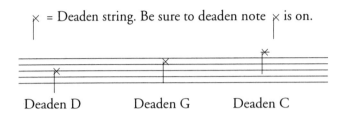

= Deaden string. Be sure to deaden note x is on.

Deaden D   Deaden G   Deaden C

Observe *accents* > and *staccato* · dots

1A

| Finger: | 2 | 2 | 1 | | 1 | 2 | 2 | 3 | 2 | 4 | | 4 | 4 | 2 | 2 | | 4 | | 3 | 2 | 1 | | 2 |
| Fret: | 5 | 4 | 4 | | | 5 | | 6 | 5 | 7 | | 7 | | | | 5 | | 7 | | 6 | 5 | 4 | 5 |

Practice study 1A slowly at first, carefully hitting all of the accents and staccatos.
Gradually work up to the tempo of: ♩= **108** on 1B

1B

2A

| Finger: | 4 | 1 | 2 | 2 | 2 | 3 | 3 | 4 | 4 | 2 | 4 | 4 | 4 |

| Fret: | 5 | 2 | 3 | | 4 | | 5 | | 3 | 5 | 5 |

2B

♩= **96** to **132**

♩= **108** to **132**

| Finger: | 2 | 1 | 2 | 2 | 2 | 3 | 3 | 4 | 2 | 2 | 3 | 4 | 2 | 2 | 4 | 3 | 3 | 2 | 2 | 1 | 1 | 2 | 2 |
| Fret: | 5 | 4 | 5 | | 6 | | 7 | 6 | 5 | 6 | 7 | 5 | | 7 | 6 | | 5 | | 5 | 3 | 4 | 5 |

Great Music at Your Fingertips